Gretchen Bitterlin
Dennis Johnson
Donna Price
Sylvia Ramirez
K. Lynn Savage, Series Editor

Add Ventures 4
MULTILEVEL WORKSHEETS

with **Ingrid Wisniewska**

CAMBRIDGE
UNIVERSITY PRESS

CAMBRIDGE UNIVERSITY PRESS
Cambridge, New York, Melbourne, Madrid, Cape Town, Singapore, São Paulo, Delhi, Dubai, Tokyo

Cambridge University Press
32 Avenue of the Americas, New York, NY 10013–2473, USA

www.cambridge.org
Information on this title: www.cambridge.org/9780521675864

First published 2009
3rd printing 2010

Printed in the United States of America

A catalog record for this publication is available from the British Library.

ISBN 978-0-521-60098-9 pack consisting of Student's Book and Audio CD
ISBN 978-0-521-67961-9 Workbook
ISBN 978-0-521-72105-9 pack consisting of Teacher's Edition and Teacher's Toolkit Audio CD / CD-ROM
ISBN 978-0-521-67732-5 CDs (Audio)
ISBN 978-0-521-67733-2 Cassettes
ISBN 978-0-521-67586-4 Add Ventures

Art direction, book design, photo research, and layout services: Adventure House, NYC
Layout services: TSI Graphics, Effingham, IL

Contents

Introduction

What is *Add Ventures*?

Add Ventures 4 is a book of reproducible worksheets to accompany the *Ventures* Student's Book 4. The worksheets give students additional practice for each lesson in the Student's Book at three levels of difficulty, making it the ideal supplemental material for multilevel classrooms.

For each two-page lesson in the Student's Book, there are three *Add Ventures* worksheets. Each worksheet is designed to provide up to 30 minutes of student work.

What are the three levels of difficulty in *Add Ventures*?

The three tiers in *Add Ventures* allow students who are in the same class but at different levels of English ability to gain confidence and proficiency through level-appropriate tasks.

☑■■ Tier 1 tasks are controlled exercises targeted at students who need the most support as they progress through the Student's Book. A major goal of Tier 1 tasks is to build students' confidence as they work.

■☑■ Tier 2 tasks target students for whom the level of the Student's Book is just right. The exercises are similar to those in the main text. The goal of Tier 2 is to provide additional on-level practice.

■■☑ Tier 3 tasks provide the least support and the greatest challenge. They require more production with fewer cues, and they may extend the content of the lesson in the Student's Book. These tasks target students who move quickly and can easily make connections with previously learned content. The goal of Tier 3 is to challenge students beyond the tasks in the Student's Book.

How do I use *Add Ventures*?

The three tiers of tasks can be structured for *like-ability* (homogeneous) or *cross-ability* (heterogeneous) groups.

In like-ability groupings, students at the *same ability level* work on the same tasks. That is, those students needing the most support work together on Tier 1; students needing the least support work together on Tier 3; students needing more on-level practice work together on Tier 2.

The same or similar content in the tasks across the three tiers of each lesson makes correction easy. Teachers can bring the students together as a whole class to review the answers because the answers on the three worksheets are the same across the tiers.

In cross-ability groupings, students at *different ability levels* work together but use their own level worksheet. Strong students and less strong students work together, enabling peer teaching and peer correction. With cross-ability groupings, the class is usually divided into two groups rather than three. That is, Tier 3 students may work with Tier 1 students while Tier 2 students work in their like-ability group; or Tier 2 students may work with Tier 1 students while Tier 3 students work in their like-ability group. With this cross-ability grouping, feedback on tasks is most often done within the group (student-to-student) rather than as a whole-class activity.

How is *Add Ventures* different from the Workbook for *Ventures*?

The **Workbook** is designed for independent student use outside of class, although it can also be used as additional in-class practice. It provides reinforcement activities at the same level as the lessons in the Student's Book.

Add Ventures is intended for in-class use, particularly in multilevel settings, to target the exercises specific to a student's language-ability level.

Add Ventures worksheets can be used after each lesson in the Student's Book or in conjunction with the Workbook.

Use the Workbook exercises first to determine the appropriate tier of *Add Ventures* to assign to each student. Or use *Add Ventures* first to address individual needs of students prior to assigning the Workbook. In this case, determine the worksheet tier for each student based on the student's understanding of the material in the Student's Book. After successful completion of their *Add Ventures* worksheets, students can do the exercises in the Workbook, either as additional classroom practice or as homework.

Lesson A *Get ready*

A Circle the correct words.

1. Peter is good at solving problems. He is (**mathematical**)/ **mechanical**.

2. Gino is good at singing. He is **musical** / **mathematical**.

3. Jasmin won a poetry contest. She is **gifted in math** / **gifted in language**.

4. Andy is good at fixing up cars. He is **mechanical** / **musical**.

5. Jan is good at making delicious dinners. He **has an aptitude for cooking** / **is a brain**.

6. Olga is good at everything. She's very **bright** / **different**.

B Complete the conversation.

Wow! Can you fix up my car?	Hi, Frankie, How's everything? You look depressed.
Sure! No problem.	I'm terrible at math, too. I'm more gifted in language.

Pete *Hi, Frankie. How's everything? You look depressed.*

Frankie Hi, Pete. Yeah, I got an F on my math test. I'm not very mathematical.

Pete _____ What about you?

Frankie I'm a mechanical person. I like finding out how machines work and fixing them.

Pete _____

Frankie OK! Can you help me with my English homework?

Pete _____

C Answer the questions. Write the letters.

a. count numbers	c. make things	e. sing
b. fix up cars	d. play an instrument	f. solve problems

1. What do mathematical people usually do well? _a_ , _____

2. What do mechanical people usually do well? _____ , _____

3. What do musical people usually do well? _____ , _____

D Complete the sentence with information about yourself.

Example: I'm good at *learning new languages* .

I'm good at _____ .

Name: _____

Lesson A *Get ready*

A Complete the sentences.

| aptitude | bright | gifted in | mathematical | mechanical | musical |

1. Peter is good at solving problems. He is *mathematical* .

2. Gino is good at singing. He is _____ .

3. Jasmin won a poetry contest. She is _____ language.

4. Andy is good at fixing up cars. He is _____ .

5. Jan is good at making delicious dinners. He has an _____ for cooking.

6. Olga is good at everything. She's very _____ .

B Number the sentences in the correct order to make a conversation.

_____ I'm terrible at math, too. I'm more gifted in language. What about you?

_____ Sure! No problem.

_1_ Hi, Frankie. How's everything? You look depressed.

_____ Wow! Can you fix up my car?

_____ Hi, Pete. Yeah, I got an F on my math test. I'm not very mathematical.

_____ OK! Can you help me with my English homework?

_____ I'm a mechanical person. I like finding out how machines work and fixing them.

C Answer the questions.

| count numbers | make things | sing |
| fix up cars | play an instrument | solve problems |

1. What do mathematical people usually do well? *Count numbers* and _____ .

2. What do mechanical people usually do well? _____ and _____ .

3. What do musical people usually do well? _____ and _____ .

D Complete the sentences with information about yourself.

Example: I'm good at *learning new languages* .

1. I'm good at _____ .

2. I'm gifted in _____ .

Lesson A Get ready

A Complete the sentences.

1. Peter is good at solving problems. He is m _a_ _t_ _h_ _e_ _m_ _a_ _t_ _i_ _c_ _a_ _l_ .

2. Gino is good at singing. He is m __ __ __ __ __ l.

3. Jasmin won a poetry contest. She is g __ __ __ __ d in language.

4. Andy is good at fixing up cars. He is m __ __ __ __ __ __ __ __ l.

5. Jan is good at making delicious dinners. He has an a __ __ __ __ __ __ e for cooking.

6. Olga is good at everything. She's very b __ __ __ __ t.

B Complete the sentences. Then number them in the correct order to make a conversation.

fix up	gifted	mathematical	mechanical

____ I'm terrible at math, too. I'm more _____ in language. What about you?

____ Sure! No problem.

_1_ Hi, Frankie. How's everything? You look depressed.

____ Wow! Can you _____ my car?

____ Hi, Pete. Yeah, I got an F on my math test. I'm not very _____ .

____ OK! Can you help me with my English homework?

____ I'm a _____ person. I like finding out how machines work and fixing them.

C Answer the questions.

count numbers	make things	sing
fix up cars	play an instrument	solve problems

1. What do mathematical people usually do well? _Count numbers and_ _____ .

2. What do mechanical people usually do well? _____ .

3. What do musical people usually do well? _____ .

D Complete the sentences with information about yourself.

Example: I'm good at _learning new languages_ .

1. I'm good at _____ .

2. I'm gifted in _____ .

3. I have an aptitude for _____ .

A Write questions. Use noun clauses.

1. Computer skills are important for everyone.

   Do you think that *computer skills are important for everyone* _____ ?

2. Science is more important than art.

   Do people believe that _____ ?

3. You need mechanical skills to fix up a car.

   Do you suppose that _____ ?

4. Everyone has some musical skills.

   Do you believe that _____ ?

5. It is important to learn grammar.

   Do you feel that _____ ?

6. More education helps people get better jobs.

   Do you think that _____ ?

B Correct the mistake in each sentence. Each mistake is <u>underlined</u>.

1. Jean thinks that <u>is Aimee</u> good at singing.

2. <u>Are</u> you believe that mathematical skills are important?

3. Everyone <u>is knowing</u> that education is important.

4. Do you think that I _____ good at dancing?

5. Frank <u>realize</u> that he has an aptitude for science.

C Choose a topic. Write a question. Then write your answer.

computer skills   mechanical skills   musical skills

Example:

Question: Do you think that *musical skills are important* ?

Answer: *Yes, I think that we need musical skills to enjoy music.*

Question: Do you think that _____ ?

Answer: _____

Lesson **B** *Noun clauses*

A Write questions. Use *that* and a noun clause.

1. Computer skills are important for everyone. (Do you think . . . ?)
   Do you think that computer skills are important for everyone?

2. Science is more important than art. (Do people believe . . . ?)
   _____

3. You need mechanical skills to fix up a car. (Do you suppose . . . ?)
   _____

4. Everyone has some musical skills. (Do you believe . . . ?)
   _____

5. It is important to learn grammar. (Do you feel . . . ?)
   _____

6. More education helps people get better jobs. (Do you think . . . ?)
   _____

B Correct the mistake in each sentence.

1. Jean thinks that is Aimee good at singing.

2. Are you believe that mathematical skills are important?

3. Everyone is knowing that education is important.

4. Do you think that I good at dancing?

5. Frank realize that he has an aptitude for science.

C Choose two topics. Write two questions. Then write your answers.

computer skills   mechanical skills   musical skills

Example: Do you think that *musical skills are important* ?
Yes, I think that we need musical skills to enjoy music.

1. Do you think that _____ ?
   _____

2. Do you believe that _____ ?
   _____

A Write questions. Use *that* and a noun clause.

1. Computer skills are important for everyone.

   (you / think) _Do you think that computer skills are important for everyone?_

2. Science is more important than art.

   (people / believe) _____

3. You need mechanical skills to fix up a car.

   (you / suppose) _____

4. Everyone has some musical skills.

   (you / believe) _____

5. It is important to learn grammar.

   (you / feel) _____

6. More education helps people get better jobs.

   (you / think) _____

B Correct the mistakes. There are two mistakes in each sentence.

1. Jean think that is Aimee good at singing.

2. Are you believe that mathematical skills is important?

3. Everyone is knowing that education are important.

4. Are you think that I good at dancing?

5. Frank realize that he have an aptitude for science.

C Choose two topics. Write two questions to ask a partner. Then write
your partner's answers.

| computer skills   mechanical skills   musical skills |

Example: _Do you think that musical skills are important?_
Sandra thinks that musical skills are important. We need them to enjoy music.

1. (think) _____

   _____

2. (believe) _____

   _____

Lesson C *Parts of speech*

Name: _____

☑ ■ ■

A Complete the chart.

Adjective	Adverb
1. skillful	*skillfully*
2. easy	
3. bad	
4.	well
5. fast	

B Circle the correct words.

1. We played very **bad** / **badly** in the soccer game, and we lost.

2. Joe got 100 percent on the test because it was very **easy** / **easily**.

3. My brother is a very **slow** / **slowly** driver.

4. Sharon talks very **quick** / **quickly**, and I can't always understand her.

5. Daniela never makes mistakes. She checks her work very **careful** / **carefully**.

6. Henrietta lived in France for many years, and she speaks French **perfect** / **perfectly**.

C Complete the chart with information about yourself. Then complete the sentences.

cook	dance	play guitar	speak English	write

Well	Not well	Skillfully
dance		

Example: I __*dance*__ well.

1. I _____ well.

2. I don't _____ well.

3. I _____ skillfully.

Lesson C *Parts of speech*

A Complete the chart.

Adjective	Adverb	Adjective	Adverb
1. skillful	*skillfully*	5. fast	
2. easy		6.	clearly
3. bad		7. perfect	
4.	well	8.	beautifully

B Complete the sentences with the correct form of the word in parentheses.

1. We played very _____*badly*_____ in the soccer game, and we lost.
   (bad)

2. Joe got 100 percent on the test because it was very _____ .
   (easy)

3. My brother is a very _____ driver.
   (slow)

4. Sharon talks very _____ , and I can't always understand her.
   (quick)

5. Daniela never makes mistakes. She checks her work very _____ .
   (careful)

6. Henrietta lived in France for many years, and she speaks French

   _____ .
   (perfect)

C Complete the chart with information about yourself. Then write sentences. Use the information in the chart.

cook	dance	play guitar	speak English	write	(your own ideas)

Well	Not well	Skillfully
dance		

Example: *I dance well.*

1. _____

2. _____

3. _____

Lesson C Parts of speech

■■■☑

A Complete the chart. Add two more pairs of adjectives and adverbs.

Adjective	Adverb	Adjective	Adverb
1. skillful	*skillfully*	6.	clearly
2. easy		7. perfect	
3. bad		8.	beautifully
4.	well	9.	
5. fast		10.	

B Complete the sentences with the correct form of the word.

bad	careful	easy	perfect	quick	slow

1. We played very _____*badly*_____ in the soccer game, and we lost.

2. Joe got 100 percent on the test because it was very _____ .

3. My brother is a very _____ driver.

4. Sharon talks very _____ , and I can't always understand her.

5. Daniela never makes mistakes. She checks her work very _____ .

6. Henrietta lived in France for many years, and she speaks French _____ .

C Complete the chart with information about yourself. Then write sentences.
Use the information in the chart.

cook	dance	play guitar	speak English	write	(your own ideas)

Well	Not well	Skillfully	Quickly
dance			

Example: _I dance well._

1. _____

2. _____

3. _____

4. _____

Name: _____

Lesson **D** *Reading*

A Circle the correct word for the definition.

1. good with words — (verbal)/ visual
2. good at solving puzzles — interpersonal / logical
3. gifted in singing or playing an instrument — verbal / musical
4. good at seeing or drawing pictures — visual / intrapersonal
5. likes to move around — logical / kinesthetic
6. good at communicating — interpersonal / visual
7. understands their own feelings — intrapersonal / musical
8. skillful with plants and animals — kinesthetic / naturalist

B Read the title of the article and the headings in **bold**. What is this article about?

a. what you do at home   b. what you are good at and enjoy   c. what your job is

C Read the article. Match the numbers in the text with the words in Exercise A.

What Types of Intelligence Do You Have?

The theory of multiple intelligences says that all of us have a variety of different types of intelligence. How do we find out what they are? Think about different aspects of your life: school, work, home, and free time. Try to identify the things you are good at and enjoy most.

At school: (1) Do you like to read and write and talk about your opinions? (2) Do you prefer to work with other students and discuss things in groups?

At work: (3) Do you like figuring out how things work and solving problems? (4) Do you like creating new images and designs?

At home: (5) Do you like listening to CDs while you cook or clean? (6) Do you prefer to spend time alone quietly thinking about your feelings?

In your free time: (7) Do you enjoy taking care of pets or looking after your garden? (8) Are you good at sports or dancing?

---

1. _____verbal_____   4. _____   7. _____
2. _____   5. _____musical_____   8. _____kinesthetic_____
3. _____logical_____   6. _____

D Complete the sentence with information about yourself.

Example: I like *talking to people* . I am *verbal* .

I like _____ . I am _____ .
            (activity)   (type of intelligence)

Lesson **D** *Reading*

■ ☑ ■

A Match the words with their definitions.

1. verbal _c_
2. logical ____
3. musical ____
4. visual ____
5. kinesthetic ____
6. interpersonal ____
7. intrapersonal ____
8. naturalist ____

a. good at seeing or drawing pictures
b. good at communicating
c. good with words
d. understands their own feelings
e. good at solving puzzles
f. likes to move around
g. skillful with plants and animals
h. gifted in singing or playing an instrument

B Read the title of the article and the headings in **bold**. What is this article about?

a. what you do at home   b. what you are good at and enjoy   c. what your job is

C Read the article. Match the numbers in the text with the words in Exercise A.

What Types of Intelligence Do You Have?

The theory of multiple intelligences says that all of us have a variety of different types of intelligence. How do we find out what they are? Think about different aspects of your life: school, work, home, and free time. Try to identify the things you are good at and enjoy most.

At school: (1) Do you like to read and write and talk about your opinions? (2) Do you prefer to work with other students and discuss things in groups?

At work: (3) Do you like figuring out how things work and solving problems? (4) Do you like creating new images and designs?

At home: (5) Do you like listening to CDs while you cook or clean? (6) Do you prefer to spend time alone quietly thinking about your feelings?

In your free time: (7) Do you enjoy taking care of pets or looking after your garden? (8) Are you good at sports or dancing?

---

1. _____*verbal*_____
2. _____
3. _____
4. _____
5. _____*musical*_____
6. _____
7. _____
8. _____

D Write sentences about intelligences you have. Use the back of this paper.

Example: _I like talking to people_ . _I am verbal_ .

Lesson D Reading

A Write the words for the definitions.

1. v _erbal_ : good with words
2. l_____ : good at solving puzzles
3. m_____ : gifted in singing or playing an instrument
4. v_____ : good at seeing or drawing pictures
5. k_____ : likes to move around
6. i_____ : good at communicating
7. i_____ : understands their own feelings
8. n_____ : skillful with plants and animals

B Read the title of the article and the headings in **bold**. What is this article about?

a. what you do at home   b. what you are good at and enjoy   c. what your job is

C Read the article. Match the numbers in the text with the words in Exercise A.

What Types of Intelligence Do You Have?

The theory of multiple intelligences says that all of us have a variety of different types of intelligence. How do we find out what they are? Think about different aspects of your life: school, work, home, and free time. Try to identify the things you are good at and enjoy most.
At school: (1) Do you like to read and write and talk about your opinions? (2) Do you prefer to work with other students and discuss things in groups?
At work: (3) Do you like figuring out how things work and solving problems? (4) Do you like creating new images and designs?
At home: (5) Do you like listening to CDs while you cook or clean? (6) Do you prefer to spend time alone quietly thinking about your feelings?
In your free time: (7) Do you enjoy taking care of pets or looking after your garden? (8) Are you good at sports or dancing?

1. _____ _verbal_ _____   4. _____   7. _____

2. _____   5. _____   8. _____

3. _____   6. _____

D Write sentences about intelligences you have and don't have. Use the back of this paper.

Example: _I like talking to people. I am verbal._
I don't like counting numbers. I am not mathematical.

Lesson E Writing

A Read the sentences. Match them with the topic sentences below. Write the numbers below each picture.

My primary intelligence is visual.

__3__ , __7__ , _____

My strongest intelligence is interpersonal.

_____ , _____ , _____

My main intelligence is intrapersonal.

__1__ , _____ , _____

1. I don't mind spending time alone.
2. I get my best ideas from talking with other people.
3. I learn best when we watch videos in class or when the teacher brings in pictures.
4. I need time to reflect on my work and think about how to improve.
5. I usually need time to make a decision.
6. I'm good at communicating with people.
7. I use diagrams in my notebooks to organize information.
8. I've always had an aptitude for art.
9. In class, I love talking with other students and discussing our opinions.

B Do any of the sentences above describe a friend? Complete the topic sentence.

My friend's primary intelligence is _____ .

C Write a paragraph about your friend and his or her primary intelligence. Use the topic sentence from Exercise B. Use sentences from Exercise A for ideas.

_____

_____

_____

_____

_____

_____

_____

Name: _____

Lesson E Writing

A Read the sentences. Match them with the topic sentences below. Write the numbers below each picture.

My primary intelligence is visual.

__3__ , __7__ , __8__ , ___

My strongest intelligence is interpersonal.

___ , ___ , ___ , ___

My main intelligence is intrapersonal.

__1__ , ___ , ___ , ___

1. I don't mind spending time alone.
2. I get my best ideas from talking with other people.
3. I learn best when we watch videos in class or when the teacher brings in pictures.
4. I need time to reflect on my work and think about how to improve.
5. I usually need time to make a decision.
6. I'm good at communicating with people.
7. I use diagrams in my notebooks to organize information.
8. I've always had an aptitude for art.
9. In class, I love talking with other students and discussing our opinions.
10. In the future, I want to be a counselor.
11. On weekends, I like to go to the park and draw pictures.
12. I don't like joining in group discussions.

B Do any of the sentences above describe a friend? Complete the topic sentence.

My friend's primary intelligence is _____ .

C Write a paragraph about your friend and his or her primary intelligence. Use the topic sentence from Exercise B. Use sentences from Exercise A for ideas.

_____

_____

_____

_____

_____

_____

Lesson E *Writing*

A Read the sentences. Match them with the topic sentences below. Write the numbers below each picture.

My primary intelligence
is visual.

__3__ , __7__ , __8__ , ____ ,

____

My strongest intelligence
is interpersonal.

____ , ____ , ____ , ____ ,

____

My main intelligence
is intrapersonal.

__1__ , ____ , ____ , ____ ,

____

1. I don't mind spending time alone.
2. I get my best ideas from talking with other people.
3. I learn best when we watch videos in class or when the teacher brings in pictures.
4. I need time to reflect on my work and think about how to improve.
5. I usually need time to make a decision.
6. I'm good at communicating with people.
7. I use diagrams in my notebooks to organize information.
8. I've always had an aptitude for art.
9. In class, I love talking with other students and discussing our opinions.
10. In the future, I want to be a counselor.
11. On weekends, I like to go to the park and draw pictures.
12. I don't like joining in group discussions.
13. When I read a story, it is easy for me to imagine what is happening.
14. I write in my journal about what happens every day.
15. In my free time, I go out with my friends or cook for them at home.

B Do any of the sentences above describe a friend? Complete the topic sentence.

My friend's primary intelligence is _____ .

C Write a paragraph about your friend and his or her primary intelligence on a separate piece of paper. Use the topic sentence from Exercise B. Use sentences from Exercise A for ideas. Add more ideas of your own.

Lesson F Another view

A Solve the puzzles.

Brainteaser Quiz

1. Unscramble the letters. What is the word?

   brevla   __ __ __ __ __ __

2. Move one X one space to make two rows of three Xs.

	X	
	X	
X		X
	X	

3. Use this code to find the word: a=3, c=9, d=8, e=4, i=0, n=1, p=2, l=5, r=6, t=7

   83194   _____

4. Which word has the same vowel sound?

   brain → game / pair

5. Take five coins out of your wallet. Hold them in your hand. Put three on the table. Take away two from the table and put back four. How many are in your hand?

   Answer: _____

6. Cross out the word that doesn't fit. Explain why.

   draw, paint, buy, dance

   _____

B Which puzzle did you enjoy most? _____ Which was not easy for you? _____

What does this quiz tell you about your intelligences? _____

A Solve the puzzles.

Brainteaser Quiz

1. Unscramble the letters. What are the words?

    brevla   __ __ __ __ __ __   ulsiva   __ __ __ __ __ __

2. Move one X one space to make two rows of three Xs.

    a.
	X	
	X	
X		X
	X	

    b.
	X	
X	X	X
		X

3. Use this code to find the words: a=3, c=9, d=8, e=4, i=0, n=1, p=2, l=5, r=6, t=7

    83194 _____   23017 _____

4. Which word has the same vowel sound?

    a. brain → game / pair   b. speak → learn / meet

5. Take five coins out of your wallet. Hold them in your hand. Put three on the table. Take away two from the table and put back four. How many are in your hand?

    Answer: _____

6. Cross out the word that doesn't fit. Explain why.

    a. draw, paint, buy, dance

    _____

    b. run, move, sing, walk

    _____

B Which puzzle did you enjoy most? _____ Which was not easy for you? _____

What does this quiz tell you about your intelligences? _____

A Solve the puzzles.

Brainteaser Quiz

1. Unscramble the letters. What are the words?

   brevla _ _ _ _ _ _   ulsiva _ _ _ _ _ _

   lilcoga _ _ _ _ _ _ _

2. Move one X one space to make two rows of three Xs.

   a.   b.   c.

3. Use this code to find the words: a=3, c=9, d=8, e=4, i=0, n=1, p=2, l=5, r=6, t=7

   83194 _____   23017 _____

   54361 _____

4. Which word has the same vowel sound?

   a. brain → game / pair   b. speak → learn / meet   c. time → find / think

5. Take five coins out of your wallet. Hold them in your hand. Put three on the table. Take away two from the table and put back four. How many are in your hand?

   Answer: _____

6. Cross out the word that doesn't fit. Explain why.

   a. draw, paint, buy, dance

   _____

   b. run, move, sing, walk

   _____

   c. brain, aptitude, intelligence, bright

   _____

B Which puzzle did you enjoy most? _____ Which was not easy for you? _____

What does this quiz tell you about your intelligences? _____

A Circle the answers.

1. Leticia speaks two languages. She is _____ .   (a.) bilingual   b. motivated
2. Hong wants to earn a lot of money. He needs a _____ job.   a. financial   b. high-paying
3. Nassim wants to work in the tourism _____ .   a. career   b. industry
4. A good English test score is one of the program _____ .   a. certificates   b. requirements
5. The college offers _____ to students who need money.   a. financial aid   b. internships
6. Fill out your application now. The _____ is tomorrow!   a. graduation   b. deadline

B Complete the conversation.

> You need to take three classes to get the certificate.
> Good morning. Can I help you?
> Yes, but you'll need to send it in right away. The deadline is next week.
> Which program are you interested in?
> Each class costs $450.

A *Good morning. Can I help you?*

B Yes, I'd like some information about the course requirements for one of your programs.

A Yes, of course. _____

B Hospitality and Tourism.

A _____

B How much does it cost?

A _____

B Could you send me an application, please?

A _____

_____

B OK. Thank you. Here is my address. . . .

BIG ROCK COLLEGE

C What kind of program are you interested in? Why? Choose a program from the box or use your own idea.

Business Office Technology	Child Day Care	Medical Assistant

I'm interested in a _____ program because _____

_____ .

Lesson A Get ready

A Complete the sentences.

bilingual	deadline	financial aid	high-paying	industry	requirements

1. Leticia speaks two languages. She is _bilingual_ .

2. Hong wants to earn a lot of money. He needs a _____ job.

3. Nassim wants to work in the tourism _____ .

4. A good English test score is one of the program _____ .

5. The college offers _____ to students who need money.

6. Fill out your application now. The _____ is tomorrow!

B Number the sentences in the correct order to make a conversation.

_____ Yes, of course. Which program are you interested in?

_1_ Good morning. Can I help you?

_____ Yes, I'd like some information about the course requirements for one of your programs.

_____ Each class costs $450.

_____ Yes, but you'll need to send it in right away. The deadline is next week.

_____ Hospitality and Tourism.

_____ You need to take three classes to get the certificate.

_____ Could you send me an application, please?

_____ OK. Thank you. Here is my address. . . .

_____ How much does it cost?

BIG ROCK COLLEGE ☆☆☆☆☆

C What kind of program are you interested in? Why? Choose a program from the box or use your own idea. Then write a question to ask about the program.

Business Office Technology	Child Day Care	Medical Assistant	Teacher's Aide

I'm interested in a _____ program because _____

_____ .

Question: _____ ?

Lesson A *Get ready*

Name: _____

■ ■ ☑

A Complete the sentences.

1. Leticia speaks two languages. She is b _i_ _l_ _i_ _n_ _g_ _u_ _a_ _l_.

2. Hong wants to earn a lot of money. He needs a high-p __ __ __ __ __ job.

3. Nassim wants to work in the tourism i__ __ __ __ __ __ __.

4. A good English test score is one of the program r__ __ __ __ __ __ __ __ __ __ __ __.

5. The college offers financial a__ __ to students who need money.

6. Fill out your application now. The d__ __ __ __ __ __ __ is tomorrow!

B Complete the sentences. Then number them in the correct order to make a conversation.

| application | certificate | deadline | requirements |

_____ Yes, of course. Which program are you interested in?

_1_ Good morning. Can I help you?

_____ Yes, I'd like some information about the course

_____ for one of your programs.

_____ Each class costs $450.

_____ Yes, but you'll need to send it in right away. The

_____ is next week.

_____ Hospitality and Tourism.

_____ You need to take three classes to get the

_____.

_____ Could you send me an _____ , please?

_____ OK. Thank you. Here is my address. . . .

_____ How much does it cost?

C What kind of program are you interested in? Why? Choose a program from the box or use your own idea. Then write questions to ask about the program.

| Business Office Technology | Child Day Care | Medical Assistant | Teacher's Aide |

I'm interested in a _____ program because _____

_____.

Question 1: _____

Question 2: _____

Lesson B The passive voice

A Rewrite the sentences. Use the present passive voice.

1. The college provides free computer classes in the summer.

   Free computer classes are _provided in the summer_ .

2. They hold the placement test in the library.

   The placement test is _____ .

3. Do they offer English classes, too?

   Are English classes _____ ?

4. What kind of experience do you need?

   What kind of experience is _____ ?

5. Do they provide a certificate at the end?

   Is a certificate _____ ?

6. What kind of forms do they require?

   What kind of forms are _____ ?

B Correct the mistake in each sentence. Each mistake is <u>underlined</u>.

1. Business classes <u>is</u> offered on Tuesdays and Thursdays.
   <small>are</small>

2. A placement test <u>____</u> held on the first day of class.

3. Where the admissions office <u>is</u> located?

4. Is financial aid <u>offer</u> by the college?

5. Registration <u>are</u> required before March 15.

6. What kind of career advice is <u>they</u> provided?

C Internet task: Go on the Internet. Find the Web site of a school or college near you. If you do not have access to the Internet, look for an ad in a local newspaper, magazine, or telephone directory. Write the information.

1. What is the school or college called? _____

2. Where is it located? _____

A Rewrite the sentences. Use the present passive voice.

1. The college provides free computer classes in the summer.

   Free computer classes *are provided in the summer* .

2. They hold the placement test in the library.

   The placement test _____ .

3. Do they offer English classes, too?

   _____ English classes _____ ?

4. What kind of experience do you need?

   What kind of experience _____ ?

5. Do they provide a certificate at the end?

   _____ a certificate _____ ?

6. What kind of forms do they require?

   What kind of forms _____ ?

B Correct the mistake in each sentence. Use the hint to help you.

1. Business classes is offered on Tuesdays and Thursdays. (verb)
   are

2. A placement test held on the first day of class. (verb)

3. Where the admissions office is located? (word order)

4. Is financial aid offer by the college? (verb)

5. Registration are required before March 15. (verb)

6. What kind of career advice is they provided? (extra word)

C Internet task: Go on the Internet. Find the Web site of a school or college near you. If you do not have access to the Internet, look for an ad in a local newspaper, magazine, or telephone directory. Write the information.

1. What is the school or college called? _____

2. Where is it located? _____

3. What are some programs offered? _____

Lesson B *The passive voice*

A Rewrite the sentences. Use the present passive voice.

1. The college provides free computer classes in the summer.
   Free computer classes are provided in the summer.

2. They hold the placement test in the library.
   _____

3. Do they offer English classes, too?
   _____

4. What kind of experience do you need?
   _____

5. Do they provide a certificate at the end?
   _____

6. What kind of forms do they require?
   _____

B Correct the mistake in each sentence.

1. Business classes $\overset{are}{\underset{\wedge}{is}}$ offered on Tuesdays and Thursdays.

2. A placement test held on the first day of class.

3. Where the admissions office is located?

4. Is financial aid offer by the college?

5. Registration are required before March 15.

6. What kind of career advice is they provided?

C Internet task: Go on the Internet. Find the Web site of a school or college near you. If you do not have access to the Internet, look for an ad in a local newspaper, magazine, or telephone directory. Write the information.

1. What is the school or college called? _____

2. Where is it located? _____

3. What are some programs offered? _____

4. Other information: _____

A Rewrite the sentences. Use the present passive voice with infinitives.

1. We require students to buy a textbook.

   Students are *required to buy a textbook* .

2. We expect students to attend all the classes.

   Students are _____ .

3. We advise students to register early.

   Students are _____ .

4. We tell students to meet with a tutor once a week.

   Students are _____ .

5. We encourage students to hand in their homework on time.

   Students are _____ .

6. We allow students to transfer credits from another program.

   Students are _____ .

B Complete the questions.

1. Are all students *expected to take* a placement test?
   (expect / take)

2. Is the college _____ a test score?
   (require / provide)

3. Are students _____ homework by e-mail?
   (encourage / send)

4. Am I _____ credits for work-experience programs?
   (allow / earn)

5. Are students _____ with a counselor?
   (advise / speak)

6. Is the teacher _____ advice about study problems?
   (expect / give)

C Write two questions a new student could ask at your school or college.

attend an orientation session   hand in homework   take a placement test

Example: Are students required to *take a placement test* ?

1. Are students required to _____ ?

2. Are students encouraged to _____ ?

Lesson C The passive voice

A Rewrite the sentences. Use the present passive voice with infinitives.

1. We require students to buy a textbook.

   Students _are required to buy a textbook_ .

2. We expect students to attend all the classes.

   Students _____ .

3. We advise students to register early.

   Students _____ .

4. We tell students to meet with a tutor once a week.

   Students _____ .

5. We encourage students to hand in their homework on time.

   Students _____ .

6. We allow students to transfer credits from another program.

   Students _____ .

B Underline the correct verb and complete the questions.

1. **Are** / **Is** all students _expected to take_ a placement test?
   (expect / take)

2. **Are** / **Is** the college _____ a test score?
   (require / provide)

3. **Are** / **Is** students _____ homework by e-mail?
   (encourage / send)

4. **Am** / **Are** I _____ credits for work-experience programs?
   (allow / earn)

5. **Are** / **Is** students _____ with a counselor?
   (advise / speak)

6. **Are** / **Is** the teacher _____ advice about study problems?
   (expect / give)

C Write three questions a new student could ask at your school or college.

| homework | an orientation session | a placement test | registration fees |

Example: Are students required to _take a placement test_ ?

1. Are students required to _____ ?

2. Are students encouraged to _____ ?

3. Are students expected to _____ ?

Lesson C *The passive voice*

A Complete the sentences. Then rewrite them using the present passive voice with infinitives.

1. We require students to _____*buy*_____ a textbook.

   Students are required to buy a textbook.

2. We expect students to _____ all the classes.

   _____

3. We advise students to _____ early.

   _____

4. We tell students to _____ with a tutor once a week.

   _____

5. We encourage students to _____ their homework on time.

   _____

6. We allow students to _____ credits from another program.

   _____

B Complete the questions.

1. *Are* all students *expected to take* a placement test?
   (expect / take)

2. _____ the college _____ a test score?
   (require / provide)

3. _____ students _____ homework by e-mail?
   (encourage / send)

4. _____ I _____ credits for work-experience programs?
   (allow / earn)

5. _____ students _____ with a counselor?
   (advise / speak)

6. _____ the teacher _____ advice about study problems?
   (expect / give)

C Write four questions a new student could ask at your school or college.

| a counselor | homework | an orientation session | a placement test | registration fees |

Example: Are students *required to take a placement test* ?

1. Are students _____ ?

2. Are students _____ ?

3. Are students _____ ?

4. Are students _____ ?

Lesson D Reading

A Skim the article. Find and circle:

a. the names of two people   b. the names of four places   c. three dates

---

Fulfilling Their Dream

In 1990, (Ivana) graduated from Kiev University in the Ukraine with a degree in science. She married her husband, Vacek, soon after graduation. Ivana taught classes at the university, and Vacek worked as a programmer for a small computer company. After their son was born, Ivana couldn't teach anymore, and they couldn't earn enough to live. Their parents and brothers and sisters were all unemployed and couldn't help them.

Ivana and Vacek decided to move to the United States to find better jobs. They studied hard to learn English and improve their computer skills. They studied immigration rules and filled out all the forms. They chose Chicago, Illinois, because there are a lot of computer companies there. They were determined to start a new life in the United States, but they were sad to leave their family and friends.

In 1992, Ivana and Vacek moved to the United States. Ivana's first job was in a delivery company as a junior clerk. She was told to organize the mail and the paperwork. The job was easy, and she worked quickly and cheerfully. Further education and training were provided and paid for by her company. In 1994, she was offered a job as a manager, and they moved to Houston, Texas.

Today Ivana and Vacek own a house. Vacek has his own Internet company, and their son is studying to be an engineer. In their free time, they offer free computer classes to other immigrants. They feel fortunate to live in the United States and want to help others fulfill their dreams, too.

B Read the article. Circle the answers.

1. Where are Ivana and Vacek from?

    (a.) The Ukraine.   b. Kiev University.

2. What did Ivana do before she came to the United States?

    a. She was a scientist.   b. She was a teacher.

3. Why did Ivana and Vacek decide to come to the United States?

    a. They needed more money.   b. They had many friends.

4. Why did Ivana and Vacek move to Houston?

    a. Ivana got a better job.   b. Their son went to college.

C Do you think it is difficult or easy for immigrants to fulfill their dreams in the United States? Why? Complete the sentence.

It is _____ because _____ .

A Skim the article. Find and circle:

a. the names of two people   b. the names of four places   c. three dates   d. four jobs

---

Fulfilling Their Dream

In 1990, (Ivana) graduated from Kiev University in the Ukraine with a degree in science. She married her husband, Vacek, soon after graduation. Ivana taught classes at the university, and Vacek worked as a programmer for a small computer company. After their son was born, Ivana couldn't teach anymore, and they couldn't earn enough to live. Their parents and brothers and sisters were all unemployed and couldn't help them.

Ivana and Vacek decided to move to the United States to find better jobs. They studied hard to learn English and improve their computer skills. They studied immigration rules and filled out all the forms. They chose Chicago, Illinois, because there are a lot of computer companies there. They were determined to start a new life in the United States, but they were sad to leave their family and friends.

In 1992, Ivana and Vacek moved to the United States. Ivana's first job was in a delivery company as a junior clerk. She was told to organize the mail and the paperwork. The job was easy, and she worked quickly and cheerfully. Further education and training were provided and paid for by her company. In 1994, she was offered a job as a manager, and they moved to Houston, Texas.

Today Ivana and Vacek own a house. Vacek has his own Internet company, and their son is studying to be an engineer. In their free time, they offer free computer classes to other immigrants. They feel fortunate to live in the United States and want to help others fulfill their dreams, too.

B Read the article. Circle the answers.

1. Where are Ivana and Vacek from?

   (a.) The Ukraine.   b. Kiev University.   c. Houston.

2. What did Ivana do before she came to the United States?

   a. She was a scientist.   b. She was a teacher.   c. She was a computer programmer.

3. Why did Ivana and Vacek decide to come to the United States?

   a. They needed more money.   b. They had many friends.   c. Their son was born.

4. Why did Ivana and Vacek move to Houston?

   a. Ivana got a better job.   b. Their son went to college.   c. They bought a house.

C Do you think it is difficult or easy for immigrants to fulfill their dreams in the United States? Why? Complete one of the sentences.

It is difficult because _____ .

It is easy because _____ .

Lesson D Reading

A Skim the article. Find and circle:

   a. people   b. places   c. dates   d. jobs

Fulfilling Their Dream

In 1990, Ivana graduated from Kiev University in the Ukraine with a degree in science. She married her husband, Vacek, soon after graduation. Ivana taught classes at the university, and Vacek worked as a programmer for a small computer company. After their son was born, Ivana couldn't teach anymore, and they couldn't earn enough to live. Their parents and brothers and sisters were all unemployed and couldn't help them.

Ivana and Vacek decided to move to the United States to find better jobs. They studied hard to learn English and improve their computer skills. They studied immigration rules and filled out all the forms. They chose Chicago, Illinois, because there are a lot of computer companies there. They were determined to start a new life in the United States, but they were sad to leave their family and friends.

In 1992, Ivana and Vacek moved to the United States. Ivana's first job was in a delivery company as a junior clerk. She was told to organize the mail and the paperwork. The job was easy, and she worked quickly and cheerfully. Further education and training were provided and paid for by her company. In 1994, she was offered a job as a manager, and they moved to Houston, Texas.

Today Ivana and Vacek own a house. Vacek has his own Internet company, and their son is studying to be an engineer. In their free time, they offer free computer classes to other immigrants. They feel fortunate to live in the United States and want to help others fulfill their dreams, too.

B Read the article. Read the answers. Write questions.

  1. **A** _Where are Ivana and Vacek from?_

     B Ivana and Vacek are from the Ukraine.

  2. **A** _____

     B She was a teacher before she came to the United States.

  3. **A** _____

     B Ivana and Vacek decided to come to the United States because they needed more money.

  4. **A** _____

     B Ivana and Vacek moved to Houston because Ivana got a better job.

C Do you think it is difficult or easy for immigrants to fulfill their dreams in the United States? Why?

_____

_____

Lesson **E** *Writing*

Name: _____

A Read the paragraph. Match the questions with the answers.

My Brother's Success Story

My brother, Sandy, is the most successful person I know. He is a musician. He writes music and has made two CDs. However, he had many obstacles on his road to success. When he was at school, he did not have enough money for music lessons. He worked in part-time jobs at night and on the weekend. He saved every penny to pay for clarinet lessons. Our parents did not encourage him to study music because they did not think he could be successful. His friends told him that it was a waste of time. They didn't believe in him. But Sandy believed that he could be a success. He practiced every day and passed his music exams. Then he was offered a scholarship to a music school. It took him five years, but he finally graduated. Now he plays clarinet in an orchestra. He had a dream and he never gave up!

1. What was Sandy's dream? _e_

2. What three obstacles to success did Sandy have? ____ , _f_ , ____

3. What did he do to overcome these obstacles? ____ , ____ , ____

4. Why was Sandy successful? ____

a. Because he had a dream and he never gave up.

b. He didn't have enough money for music lessons.

c. He practiced every day.

d. He saved money for music lessons.

e. He wanted to be a musician.

f. His friends didn't believe in him.

g. His parents didn't encourage him.

h. He earned a scholarship to music school.

B Circle *O* for obstacle or *S* for success.

1. Dave saved money for a new car.   O   (S)

2. Sofia passed all her exams.   O   S

3. Sam wasn't encouraged to study.   O   S

4. Luisa won a dance contest.   O   S

5. Osman graduated from business school.   O   S

6. Zhu wasn't offered a scholarship.   O   S

Lesson **E** *Writing*

A Read the paragraph. Answer the questions.

My Brother's Success Story

My brother, Sandy, is the most successful person I know. He is a musician. He writes music and has made two CDs. However, he had many obstacles on his road to success. When he was at school, he did not have enough money for music lessons. He worked in part-time jobs at night and on the weekend. He saved every penny to pay for clarinet lessons. Our parents did not encourage him to study music because they did not think he could be successful. His friends told him that it was a waste of time. They didn't believe in him. But Sandy believed that he could be a success. He practiced every day and passed his music exams. Then he was offered a scholarship to a music school. It took him five years, but he finally graduated. Now he plays clarinet in an orchestra. He had a dream and he never gave up!

---

1. What was Sandy's dream?

   He wanted to be a _____*musician*_____ .

2. What three obstacles to success did Sandy have?

   He didn't have _____ for music lessons.

   His parents didn't _____ him.

   His friends didn't _____ in him.

3. What did he do to overcome these obstacles?

   He saved _____ for music lessons.

   He _____ every day.

   He earned a _____ to music school.

4. Why was Sandy successful?

   Because he had _____ and he _____ .

B Complete the sentences. Circle *O* for obstacle or *S* for success.

1. Dave **saved** / **was saved** money for a new car.   O   Ⓢ

2. Sofia **passed** / **was passed** all her exams.   O   S

3. Sam **didn't** / **wasn't** encouraged to study.   O   S

4. Luisa **won** / **was won** a dance contest.   O   S

5. Osman **graduated** / **was graduated** from business school. O   S

6. Zhu **didn't** / **wasn't** offered a scholarship.   O   S

Name: _____

A Read the paragraph. Answer the questions.

My Brother's Success Story

My brother, Sandy, is the most successful person I know. He is a musician. He writes music and has made two CDs. However, he had many obstacles on his road to success. When he was at school, he did not have enough money for music lessons. He worked in part-time jobs at night and on the weekend. He saved every penny to pay for clarinet lessons. Our parents did not encourage him to study music because they did not think he could be successful. His friends told him that it was a waste of time. They didn't believe in him. But Sandy believed that he could be a success. He practiced every day and passed his music exams. Then he was offered a scholarship to a music school. It took him five years, but he finally graduated. Now he plays clarinet in an orchestra. He had a dream and he never gave up!

---

1. What was Sandy's dream?

   He wanted _to be a musician_____ .

2. What three obstacles to success did Sandy have?

   He didn't have _____ . His parents didn't

   _____ . His friends didn't _____ .

3. What did he do to overcome these obstacles?

   He saved _____ . He practiced

   _____ . He earned a _____ .

4. Why was Sandy successful?

   Because he had _____ .

B Complete the sentences. Then circle *O* for obstacle or *S* for success.

encouraged	graduated	offered	passed	saved	won

1. Dave _saved_ money for a new car.   O   Ⓢ

2. Sofia _____ all her exams.   O   S

3. Sam wasn't _____ to study.   O   S

4. Luisa _____ a dance contest.   O   S

5. Osman _____ from business school.   O   S

6. Zhu wasn't _____ a scholarship.   O   S

Add Ventures 4

Lesson F Another view

A Read the notice. Circle the answers to complete the sentences.

New classes at North College this semester

• **Auto Mechanics**   • **Food Service**   • **Nursing**   • **Office Systems**   • **Retail**

Classes are _____ at all locations. The admissions office is _____ in the Main Building.
1   2
Registration is _____ before May 15. The placement test is _____ in the library building
3   4
on May 18. Students are _____ to meet with a counselor before they apply.
5
Apply now!

---

1. a. located   (b.) offered

2. a. allowed   b. located

3. a. required   b. provided

4. a. held   b. required

5. a. offered   b. encouraged

B Read the clues. Complete the crossword puzzle.

Down

1. This person makes speeches.
4. This person plays soccer. He or she is a soccer _____ .
5. This person is in movies.
7. This person sings.

Across

2. This person writes books.
3. This person dances.
6. This person plays music.

Name: _____

Lesson F | Another view

A Read the notice. Circle the answers to complete the sentences.

New classes at North College this semester

• **Auto Mechanics**   • **Food Service**   • **Nursing**   • **Office Systems**   • **Retail**

Classes are ____ at all locations. The admissions office is ____ in the Main Building.
                    1   2
Registration is ____ before May 15. The placement test is ____ in the library building
                    3   4
on May 18. Students are ____ to meet with a counselor before they apply.
                          5
Apply now!

---

1. a. located   (b.) offered   c. provided

2. a. allowed   b. located   c. advised

3. a. required   b. provided   c. located

4. a. held   b. required   c. allowed

5. a. offered   b. encouraged   c. provided

B Read the clues. Complete the crossword puzzle.

Down

1. This person makes speeches.
4. This person plays soccer. He or she is a soccer ____ .
5. This person is in movies.
7. This person sings.

Across

2. This person writes books.
3. This person dances.
6. This person plays music.

Lesson F *Another view*

Name: _____

A Read the notice. Complete the sentences.

| encouraged | held | located | offered | required |

New classes at North College this semester

• **Auto Mechanics**   • **Food Service**   • **Nursing**   • **Office Systems**   • **Retail**

Classes are _____*offered*_____ at all locations. The admissions office is
₁
_____ in the Main Building. Registration is _____ before
₂   ₃
May 15. The placement test is _____ in the library building on May 18.
₄
Students are _____ to meet with a counselor before they apply.
₅
Apply now!

B Read the clues. Guess the words. Then number the clues and complete the crossword puzzle.

_____ This person writes books. _____

_1_ This person makes speeches. _____*statesman*_____

_____ This person is in movies. _____

_____ This person sings. _____

_____ This person dances. _____

_____ This person plays soccer. He or she is a soccer _____ .

_____ This person plays music. _____

Lesson A Get ready

☑ ■ ■

A Circle the answers.

1. My parents had a lot of rules. They were very ____ .   a. (strict)   b. raised
2. I can tell my friend everything because I ____ her.   a. trust   b. promise
3. We are not ____ to use cell phones in class.   a. enforced   b. permitted
4. I was born in Florida, but I was ____ in California.   a. raised   b. grounded
5. You can't go to the party alone. You need a ____ .   a. punishment   b. chaperone
6. Frieda copied her friend's homework. She ____ the rules.   a. brought   b. broke

B Complete the conversation.

break	chaperone	grounded	permitted	raising	strict

Soraya My kids say that I'm too __*strict*__ with them. Do you have rules for
your kids, Amy?

Amy Yes, we certainly do. I was brought up to understand that we need
rules, and I'm _____ my kids the same way.

Soraya Are they _____ to stay out late?

Amy No. They need to be home by 7:00 p.m. If they have a
_____ , they can stay out until 9:00 p.m., but no later.

Soraya I see. And what kind of punishment do they get if they
_____ the rules?

Amy Let's see. They are _____ for the weekend . . . or
no TV . . . or no cell phone – that's for something really serious.

Soraya You have some good ideas! I'll have to try them with my kids.

C Write an activity you were not permitted to do when you were a child. What
punishment did you get for breaking rules?

Not permitted	Punishment

Lesson A Get ready

A Complete the sentences.

1. My parents had a lot of rules. They were very __d__ .   a. chaperone
2. I can tell my friend everything because I ____ her.   b. raised
3. We are not ____ to use cell phones in class.   c. broke
4. I was born in Florida, but I was ____ in California.   d. strict
5. You can't go to the party alone. You need a ____ .   e. permitted
6. Frieda copied her friend's homework. She ____ the rules.   f. trust

B Complete the conversation.

break	chaperone	permitted	rules
brought up	grounded	raising	strict

Soraya My kids say that I'm too __strict__ with them. Do you have

_____ for your kids, Amy?

Amy Yes, we certainly do. I was _____ to understand that we

need rules, and I'm _____ my kids the same way.

Soraya Are they _____ to stay out late?

Amy No. They need to be home by 7:00 p.m. If they have a

_____ , they can stay out until 9:00 p.m., but no later.

Soraya I see. And what kind of punishment do they get if they

_____ the rules?

Amy Let's see. They are _____ for the weekend . . . or

no TV . . . or no cell phone – that's for something really serious.

Soraya You have some good ideas! I'll have to try them with my kids.

C Write two activities you were not permitted to do when you were a child. What punishment did you get for breaking rules?

Not permitted	Punishment

Name: _____

Lesson A Get ready

■ ■ ☑

A Complete the sentences.

1. My parents had a lot of rules. They were very s _t_ _r_ _i_ _c_ _t_ .

2. I can tell my friend everything because I t __ __ s __ her.

3. We are not p __ __ __ __ __ __ __ d to use cell phones in class.

4. I was born in Florida, but I was r __ __ __ __ __ in California.

5. You can't go to the party alone. You need a ch __ p __ __ o __ __ .

6. Frieda copied her friend's homework. She b __ __ k __ the rules.

B Complete the conversation.

break	chaperone	permitted	raising	stay out
brought up	grounded	punishment	rules	strict

Soraya My kids say that I'm too ___strict___ with them. Do you have

_____ for your kids, Amy?

Amy Yes, we certainly do. I was _____ to understand that we

need rules, and I'm _____ my kids the same way.

Soraya Are they _____ to _____ late?

Amy No. They need to be home by 7:00 p.m. If they have a

_____ , they can stay out until 9:00 p.m., but no later.

Soraya I see. And what kind of _____ do they get if they

_____ the rules?

Amy Let's see. They are _____ for the weekend . . . or

no TV . . . or no cell phone – that's for something really serious.

Soraya You have some good ideas! I'll have to try them with my kids.

C Write three activities you were not permitted to do when you were a child. What punishment did you get for breaking rules?

Not permitted	Punishment

Lesson B *Indirect questions*

A Circle the answers.

1. Can you tell me why   (a.) you are late?   b. are you late?

2. I'd like to know where   a. did she go last night.   b. she went last night.

3. Tell me when   a. you came home yesterday.   b. did you come home.

4. I wonder what   a. did he do yesterday.   b. he did yesterday.

5. Do you know how   a. are they feeling now?   b. they are feeling now?

6. I don't know who   a. they talked to after class.   b. did they talk with after class.

B Complete the conversations.

1. **A** Do you know what _his name is_ ?

   B His name is Jun.

2. **A** Can you tell me where _____ ?

   B The classroom is on the second floor.

3. **A** I don't know when _____ .

   B The class starts at 9:30 a.m.

4. **A** Tell me how _____ .

   B I came to school by bus this morning.

5. **A** I wonder who _____ .

   B They were talking to the teacher.

6. **A** I'd like to know why _____ .

   B She got a D because she didn't study very hard.

C Correct the sentences. Add the missing word.

1. Can you tell me when she ^went home? (went)

2. Do you know who the teacher? (is)

3. Tell me where the answers. (are)

4. I'd like to know when the test. (begins)

5. I don't know what they in English class yesterday. (did)

6. I wonder why she school early today. (left)

Lesson B Indirect questions

A Match.

1. Can you tell me why __d__   a. you came home yesterday.

2. I'd like to know where _____   b. they are feeling now?

3. Tell me when _____   c. he did yesterday.

4. I wonder what _____   d. you are late?

5. Do you know how _____   e. they talked to after class.

6. I don't know who _____   f. she went last night.

B Complete the conversations.

who	what	where	when	why	how

1. **A** Do you know _what his name is_ ?

   B His name is Jun.

2. **A** Can you tell me _____ ?

   B The classroom is on the second floor.

3. **A** I don't know _____ .

   B The class starts at 9:30 a.m.

4. **A** Tell me _____ .

   B I came to school by bus this morning.

5. **A** I wonder _____ .

   B They were talking to the teacher.

6. **A** I'd like to know _____ .

   B She got a D because she didn't study very hard.

C Correct the sentences. Add the missing word.

are	begins	did	is	left	went

                    went

1. Can you tell me when she ∧ home?

2. Do you know who the teacher?

3. Tell me where the answers.

4. I'd like to know when the test.

5. I don't know what they in English class yesterday.

6. I wonder why she school early today.

Lesson **B** *Indirect questions*

Name: _____

A Complete the sentences.

1. (Why are you late?) Can you tell me _why you are late_ ?

2. (Where did she go last night?) I'd like to know _____ .

3. (When did you come home yesterday?) Tell me _____ .

4. (What did he do yesterday?) I wonder _____ .

5. (How are they feeling now?) Do you know _____ ?

6. (Who did they talk to after class?) I don't know _____ .

B Complete the conversations.

1. **A** Do you know _what his name is_ ?

   B His name is Jun.

2. **A** Can you tell me _____ ?

   B The classroom is on the second floor.

3. **A** I don't know _____ .

   B The class starts at 9:30 a.m.

4. **A** Tell me _____ .

   B I came to school by bus this morning.

5. **A** I wonder _____ .

   B They were talking to the teacher.

6. **A** I'd like to know _____ .

   B She got a D because she didn't study very hard.

C Correct the sentences. Add the correct form of the missing verb.

be	begin	do	go	leave

1. Can you tell me when she ^went^ home?

2. Do you know who the teacher?

3. Tell me where the answers.

4. I'd like to know when the test.

5. I don't know what they in English class yesterday.

6. I wonder why she school early today.

Lesson C *Indirect questions*

Name: _____

A Rewrite the questions as indirect questions with *if*.

Class party!

You are invited to a class party on Thursday.
Starts at 6:30 p.m., 354 Kendall Street.
Dancing, music, and fun! See you there!

1. Do I need to buy a ticket? Can you tell me *if I need to buy a ticket* ?

2. Can I bring my friend? I'd like to know _____ .

3. Will all our classmates be there? I wonder _____ .

4. Is our teacher invited? Do you know _____ ?

5. Are they going to serve food? Do you know _____ ?

6. Do I need to bring soda or chips? I wonder _____ .

B Complete the conversation.

had a party last year	is this weekend
is going to be there	will be music

Sam Hi, Penny. Did you hear about the class party?

Penny No, I didn't. Do you know if it *is this weekend* ?
  ₁

Sam No, it isn't this weekend. It's on Thursday.

Penny I wonder if everyone in our class _____ .
  ₂

Sam Yes, everyone in our class is going to be there.

Penny Do you know if there _____ ?
  ₃

Sam Yes, I'm sure there will be music.

Penny Good. Do you know if they _____ ?
  ₄

Sam Yes, they had a party last year. It was fun. This party will be fun, too!

C Write a question about a celebration you want to go to.

Name of event _____

Do you know if _____ ?

Lesson C Indirect questions

A Complete the questions as indirect questions with *if*.

Class party!

You are invited to a class party on Thursday.
Starts at 6:30 p.m., 354 Kendall Street.
Dancing, music, and fun! See you there!

1. Can you tell me *if I need to buy a ticket* _____ ? (I / need / buy a ticket)
2. I'd like to know _____ . (I / can / bring / my friend)
3. I wonder _____ . (all our classmates / be there)
4. Do you know _____ ? (our teacher / be invited)
5. Do you know _____ ? (they / going to / serve food)
6. I wonder _____ . (I / need / bring / soda or chips)

B Complete the conversation. Use indirect questions with *if*.

Sam Hi, Penny. Did you hear about the class party?

Penny No, I didn't. Do you know *if it is this weekend* ?
$$_{1}$$

Sam No, it isn't this weekend. It's on Thursday.

Penny I wonder _____ .
$$_{2}$$

Sam Yes, everyone in our class is going to be there.

Penny Do you know _____ ?
$$_{3}$$

Sam Yes, I'm sure there will be music.

Penny Good. Do you know _____ last year?
$$_{4}$$

Sam Yes, they had a party last year. It was fun. This party will be fun, too!

C Write two questions about a celebration you want to go to.

Name of event _____

1. Do you know if _____ ?

2. I wonder if _____ .

Name: _____

Lesson C Indirect questions

A Complete the questions as indirect questions with *if*.

Class party!

You are invited to a class party on Thursday.
Starts at 6:30 p.m., 354 Kendall Street.
Dancing, music, and fun! See you there!

1. (I / need / buy / ticket) Can you tell me *if I need to buy a ticket* _____ ?

2. (I / can / bring / my friend) I'd like to know _____ .

3. (all our classmates / be / there) I wonder _____ .

4. (our teacher / be / invited) Do you know _____ ?

5. (they / go / serve / food) Do you know _____ ?

6. (I / need / bring / soda or chips) I wonder _____ .

B Complete the conversation. Use indirect questions with *if*.

Sam Hi, Penny. Did you hear about the class party?

Penny No, I didn't. Do you know *if it is this weekend* ?
⎯⎯⎯⎯⎯⎯⎯⎯⎯⎯⎯⎯
1

Sam No, it isn't this weekend. It's on Thursday.

Penny I wonder _____ .
2

Sam Yes, everyone in our class is going to be there.

Penny Do you know _____ ?
3

Sam Yes, I'm sure there will be music.

Penny Good. Do you know _____ last year?
4

Sam Yes, they had a party last year. It was fun. This party will be fun, too!

C Write three questions about a celebration you want to go to.

Name of event _____

1. Do you know if _____ ?

2. I wonder if _____ .

3. Can you tell me if _____ ?

Lesson D *Reading*

Name: _____

A Skim the article. Find the words in *italics*. Match the definitions with the words.

1. good at using your imagination __*b*__   a. successful

2. the process of learning _____   b. creative

3. good at doing something _____   c. different

4. to talk or speak with someone _____   d. education

5. not the same _____   e. communicate

B Read the article. Answer the questions.

Communication Barriers

People say that technology is helping us to break down communication barriers. We can *communicate* with each other anywhere in the world by e-mail. We carry cell phones with us and can talk to our family and friends any time and any place. We can get information on the Internet more quickly and easily than ever before. But can technology also be a barrier to communication?

Alicia is 49 years old. She lives with her son, Kwadjo. He is 15. Kwadjo is quiet and shy. He doesn't talk much, but he is very *creative*. He spends his free time designing video games on the computer. He's not interested in *education* at school. Alicia tries to explain to him that he needs education to be *successful* in life, but her son has *different* interests. Kwadjo and his friends speak a strange language full of new words about computers. Alicia doesn't understand what they are talking about. What is the barrier to communication between Alicia and her son – is it age, or is it technology?

1. A communication barrier is _____ .
   (a.) a problem in communication   b. an opportunity to communicate

2. E-mail, cell phones, and the Internet are all examples of _____ .
   a. technology   b. barriers

3. Kwadjo is successful at _____ .
   a. talking with his mom   b. designing video games

4. Alicia finds it difficult to talk with her son because _____ .
   a. he talks about things she doesn't understand   b. he doesn't have an education

C What else can be a communication barrier? Choose one. Give an example.

| Education   Language |

_____ can be a barrier to communication because _____

A Skim the article. Find the words in *italics*. Write each word beside its definition and circle the correct part of speech.

1. good at using your imagination: *creative*   noun / verb / (adjective)

2. the process of learning: _____   noun / verb / adjective

3. good at doing something: _____   noun / verb / adjective

4. to talk or speak with someone: _____   noun / verb / adjective

5. not the same: _____   noun / verb / adjective

B Read the article. Answer the questions.

Communication Barriers

People say that technology is helping us to break down communication barriers. We can *communicate* with each other anywhere in the world by e-mail. We carry cell phones with us and can talk to our family and friends any time and any place. We can get information on the Internet more quickly and easily than ever before. But can technology also be a barrier to communication?

Alicia is 49 years old. She lives with her son, Kwadjo. He is 15. Kwadjo is quiet and shy. He doesn't talk much, but he is very *creative*. He spends his free time designing video games on the computer. He's not interested in *education* at school. Alicia tries to explain to him that he needs education to be *successful* in life, but her son has *different* interests. Kwadjo and his friends speak a strange language full of new words about computers. Alicia doesn't understand what they are talking about. What is the barrier to communication between Alicia and her son – is it age, or is it technology?

1. A communication barrier is _____ .
   (a.) a problem in communication   b. an opportunity to communicate   c. a language

2. E-mail, cell phones, and the Internet are all examples of _____ .
   a. technology   b. barriers   c. information

3. Kwadjo is successful at _____ .
   a. talking with his mom   b. designing video games   c. school

4. Alicia finds it difficult to talk with her son because _____ .
   a. he talks about things she doesn't understand   b. he doesn't have an education
   c. he isn't interested in talking to her

C What else can be a communication barrier? Choose one. Give two examples.

| Culture   Education   Language |

_____ can be a barrier to communication because _____

Add Ventures 4   47

Lesson D *Reading*

A Skim the article. Find the words in *italics*. Write each word beside its definition and write the part of speech (noun, verb, or adjective).

1. good at using your imagination: *creative*   *adjective*

2. the process of learning: _____   _____

3. good at doing something: _____   _____

4. to talk or speak with someone: _____   _____

5. not the same: _____   _____

B Read the article. Answer the questions.

Communication Barriers

    People say that technology is helping us to break down communication barriers. We can *communicate* with each other anywhere in the world by e-mail. We carry cell phones with us and can talk to our family and friends any time and any place. We can get information on the Internet more quickly and easily than ever before. But can technology also be a barrier to communication?

    Alicia is 49 years old. She lives with her son, Kwadjo. He is 15. Kwadjo is quiet and shy. He doesn't talk much, but he is very *creative*. He spends his free time designing video games on the computer. He's not interested in *education* at school. Alicia tries to explain to him that he needs education to be *successful* in life, but her son has *different* interests. Kwadjo and his friends speak a strange language full of new words about computers. Alicia doesn't understand what they are talking about. What is the barrier to communication between Alicia and her son – is it age, or is it technology?

1. A communication barrier is _____ .
   a. a problem in communication
   b. an opportunity to communicate
   c. a language
   d. a video game

2. E-mail, cell phones, and the Internet are all examples of _____ .
   a. technology
   b. barriers
   c. information
   d. computers

3. Kwadjo is successful at _____ .
   a. talking with his mom
   b. designing video games
   c. school
   d. education

4. Alicia finds it difficult to talk with her son because _____ .
   a. he talks about things she doesn't understand
   b. he doesn't have an education
   c. he isn't interested in talking to her
   d. he doesn't speak English

C What else can be a communication barrier? Why? Choose one. Give three examples. Use the back of this paper.

Age	Culture	Education	Language

Lesson E *Writing*

Name: _____

A Look at the pictures. Complete the sentences.

| banana |
| computers |
| cookies |
| healthy food |
| junk food |
| sports |
| tennis |

One difference between Berta and her brother, Rob, is that they have different likes and dislikes. Berta likes _____*sports*_____ . For example, she plays _____ at the gym every day. In addition, she likes to eat _____ . For example, she often eats a _____ on her way to work. On the other hand, Rob is interested in _____ . He goes on the Internet every day. He likes to eat _____ . For example, he loves _____ . Berta and Rob are very different. Maybe that's why they get along so well!

B Circle the correct phrase.

1. Brian likes music. (**For example,**) / **On the other hand,** he goes to concerts every weekend.

2. Lina eats fruit every day. **For example,** / **On the other hand,** she eats ice cream only once a week.

3. Kathy loves to dance. **For example,** / **On the other hand,** she goes to dance class every week.

4. Samuel likes to keep in shape. **For example,** / **On the other hand,** he goes to the gym every day.

5. Omar loves going to the movies. **For example,** / **On the other hand,** he hates watching TV.

6. Zhu reads the newspaper every day. **For example,** / **On the other hand,** he doesn't read books often.

C Complete the sentences about differences between you and a friend.

I like _____ . For example, _____ .

On the other hand, my friend likes _____ . For example, _____

_____ .

Lesson E Writing

Name: _____

A Look at the pictures. Complete the sentences.

Berta

Rob

One difference between Berta and her brother, Rob, is that they have different likes and dislikes. Berta likes _____*sports*_____ . For example, she plays _____ at the gym every day. In addition, she likes to eat healthy food. For example, she often eats a _____ on her way to work. On the other hand, Rob is interested in _____ . He goes on the Internet every day. He likes to eat junk food. For example, he loves _____ . Berta and Rob are very different. Maybe that's why they get along so well!

B Complete the sentences. Use *For example* or *On the other hand*.

1. Brian likes music. _*For example*_ , he goes to concerts every weekend.

2. Lina eats fruit every day. _____ , she eats ice cream only once a week.

3. Kathy loves to dance. _____ , she goes to dance class every week.

4. Samuel likes to keep in shape. _____ , he goes to the gym every day.

5. Omar loves going to the movies. _____ , he hates watching TV.

6. Zhu reads the newspaper every day. _____ , he doesn't read books often.

C Complete the sentences about differences between you and a friend.

I like _____ . For example, _____

_____ and _____ .

On the other hand, my friend likes _____ . For example, _____

_____ and _____ .

Lesson E *Writing*

A Look at the pictures. Complete the sentences.

Berta

Rob

One difference between Berta and her brother, Rob, is that they have different

likes and dislikes. Berta likes _____*sports*_____ . For example, she plays

_____ at the gym every day. In addition, she likes to eat healthy food.

For example, she often eats a _____ on her way to work. She loves to

wear nice _____ . For example, she often wears a _____

to work. On the other hand, Rob is interested in _____ . He goes

on the Internet every day. He likes to eat junk food. For example, he loves

_____ . He usually wears _____ and a _____ .

Berta and Rob are very different. Maybe that's why they get along so well!

B Complete the sentences. Use transitions.

1. Brian likes music. _*For example*_ , he goes to concerts every weekend.

2. Lina eats fruit every day. _On the other hand_ , she eats ice cream
   only once a week.

3. Kathy loves to dance. _____ , she goes to
   dance class every week.

4. Samuel likes to keep in shape. _____ , he goes
   to the gym every day.

5. Omar loves going to the movies. _____ , he hates
   watching TV.

6. Zhu reads the newspaper every day. _____ , he doesn't read
   books often.

C Write a paragraph about differences between you and a friend. Use a separate
piece of paper.

Lesson F *Another view*

A Read the information in the chart. Answer the questions.

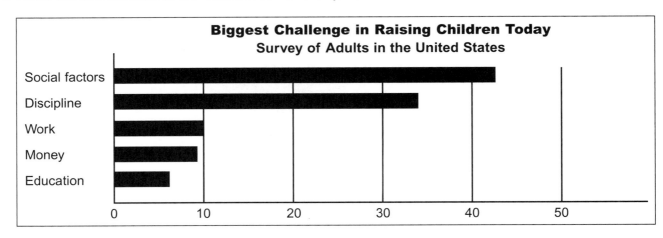

1. What was the population surveyed in this study?
   a. children in the U.S.   b. adults in the U.S.

2. What percentage of people said that social factors were the biggest challenge?
   a. 42 percent   b. 33 percent

3. What did 6 percent of people say was the biggest challenge?
   a. work   b. education

4. Which of the following is true?
   a. More people chose work than discipline.   b. More people chose money than education.

B Read the information about the teenagers. Write the names in the chart.

Names	Go to the mall with friends	Stay out after 8:00 p.m.	Go out on a date with a chaperone	Spend the night at a friend's house	Have a cell phone
Sheena	✔	✔	✔	✘	✘
	✔	✘	✔	✔	✘
	✘	✘	✘	✘	✔
	✘	✔	✘	✘	✔

What are Sheena, Martin, Diana, and Jimmy permitted to do?

1. Sheena is permitted to go to the mall with friends. She isn't permitted to spend the night at a friend's house.
2. Martin is permitted to stay out after 8:00 p.m.
3. Diana is not permitted to stay out after 8:00 p.m.
4. Jimmy is not permitted to spend the night at a friend's house.
5. Sheena and Diana are permitted to go out on a date with a chaperone.

Lesson F *Another view*

A Read the information in the chart. Answer the questions.

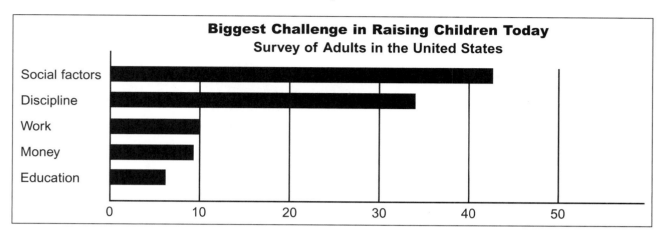

Biggest Challenge in Raising Children Today
Survey of Adults in the United States

1. What was the population surveyed in this study?
   a. children in the U.S.   (b.) adults in the U.S.   c. mothers in the U.S.

2. What percentage of people said that social factors were the biggest challenge?
   a. 42 percent   b. 33 percent   c. 9 percent

3. What did 6 percent of people say was the biggest challenge?
   a. work   b. education   c. money

4. Complete the sentence:
   More people chose money than _____ .

B Read the information about the teenagers. Write the names in the chart.

What are Sheena, Martin, Diana, and Jimmy permitted to do?					
Names	Go to the mall with friends	Stay out after 8:00 p.m.	Go out on a date with a chaperone	Spend the night at a friend's house	Have a cell phone
Sheena	✔	✔	✔	✘	✘
	✔	✘	✔	✔	✘
	✘	✘	✘	✘	✔
	✘	✔	✘	✘	✔

1. Sheena is permitted to go to the mall with friends. She isn't permitted to spend the night at a friend's house.
2. Martin is permitted to stay out after 8:00 p.m.
3. Diana is not permitted to stay out after 8:00 p.m.
4. Jimmy is not permitted to spend the night at a friend's house.
5. Sheena and Diana are permitted to go out on a date with a chaperone.
6. Martin and Jimmy are permitted to have a cell phone.

A Read the information in the chart. Answer the questions.

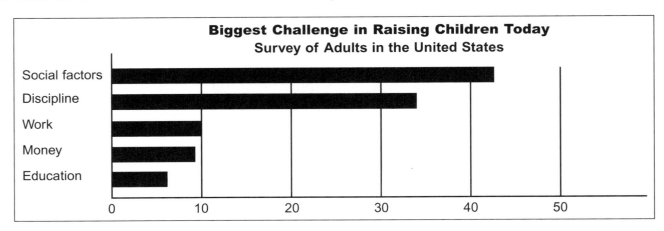

Biggest Challenge in Raising Children Today
Survey of Adults in the United States

1. What was the population surveyed in this study? *adults in the U.S.*

2. What percentage of people said that social factors were the biggest challenge? _____

3. What did 6 percent of people say was the biggest challenge? _____

4. Which of the following is true?
   a. More people chose work than discipline.
   b. More people chose money than education.
   c. More people chose discipline than social factors.

B Read the information about the teenagers. Write the names in the chart.

What are Sheena, Martin, Diana, and Jimmy permitted to do?					
Names	Go to the mall with friends	Stay out after 8:00 p.m.	Go out on a date with a chaperone	Spend the night at a friend's house	Have a cell phone
Sheena	✔	✔	✔	✘	✘
	✔	✘	✔	✔	✘
	✘	✘	✘	✘	✔
	✘	✔	✘	✘	✔

1. Sheena is permitted to go to the mall with friends. She isn't permitted to spend the night at a friend's house.

2. Martin is permitted to stay out after 8:00 p.m.

3. Diana is not permitted to stay out after 8:00 p.m.

4. Jimmy is not permitted to spend the night at a friend's house.

5. Sheena and Diana are permitted to go out on a date with a chaperone.

6. Martin and Jimmy are permitted to have a cell phone.

7. Only Diana is permitted to spend the night at a friend's house.

A Circle the answers.

1. I feel upset and angry. I need to _____ .   (a.) calm down   b. concentrate

2. Ariana feels nervous. She has a lot of _____ .   a. anxiety   b. advice

3. I have too much work to do. I feel _____ out.   a. worried   b. stressed

4. One way to relax is to practice deep _____ .   a. thinking   b. breathing

5. Lee has an exam. He feels nervous and _____ .   a. tense   b. positive

6. Meditation is one way to _____ stress.   a. concentrate   b. cope with

B Complete the ad.

anxiety	breathing	calm down	cope with	stressed	tense

Meditation Class

Do you feel ____*stressed*____ out? Do you feel worried and _____ every day? Do you have trouble sleeping or concentrating at work? These are symptoms of stress in your life.

Learn how to _____ stress in our easy meditation class. Learn techniques for deep _____ and thinking positive thoughts. Just ten minutes each day can help you _____ and relax. Learn to reduce _____ . You'll enjoy life more!

Classes start January 15. Call (304) 555-5689 to find out more.

C Match the questions and the answers. Use the information from Exercise B.

1. Who is this class for? _*b*_

2. What are two symptoms of stress? _____

3. What are two techniques you learn in the class? _____

4. What can meditation help you to do? _____

5. Do you want to take this class? Why or why not? _____

a. Deep breathing and positive thinking.

b. People who feel stressed out.

c. Calm down and relax.

d. You can't sleep and you can't concentrate.

A Complete the sentences.

anxiety	breathing	calm down	cope with	stressed	tense

1. I feel upset and angry. I need to _____*calm down*_____ .

2. Ariana feels nervous. She has a lot of _____ .

3. I have too much work to do. I feel _____ out.

4. One way to relax is to practice deep _____ .

5. Lee has an exam. He feels nervous and _____ .

6. Meditation is one way to _____ stress.

B Complete the ad. Use the words from Exercise A.

Meditation Class

Do you feel _____*stressed*_____ out? Do you feel
worried and _____ every day? Do you
have trouble sleeping or concentrating at work? These
are symptoms of stress in your life.

Learn how to _____ stress in our easy meditation class. Learn
techniques for deep _____ and thinking positive thoughts. Just
ten minutes each day can help you _____ and relax. Learn to
reduce _____ . You'll enjoy life more!

Classes start January 15. Call (304) 555-5689 to find out more.

C Answer the questions. Use the information from Exercise B.

1. Who is this class for? People who feel *stressed out* .

2. What are two symptoms of stress? You can't _____ and you can't

   _____ .

3. What are two techniques you learn in the class? Deep _____ and

   _____ thinking.

4. What can meditation help you to do? Calm _____ and _____ .

5. Do you want to take this class? Why or why not? _____

_____

A Complete the sentences.

1. I feel upset and angry. I need to c <u>a</u> <u>l</u> <u>m</u> <u>d</u> <u>o</u> <u>w</u> n.

2. Ariana feels nervous. She has a lot of a__ __ __ __ __y.

3. I have too much work to do. I feel s__ __ __ __ __ __d out.

4. One way to relax is to practice deep b__ __ __ __ __ __ __g.

5. Lee has an exam. He feels nervous and t__ __ __e.

6. Meditation is one way to c__ __e w__ __ __ stress.

B Complete the ad. Use the words from Exercise A and the words in the box.

| concentrating   meditation   symptoms |

Meditation Class

Do you feel _____*stressed*_____ out? Do you feel

worried and _____ every day? Do you

have trouble sleeping or _____ at work?

These are _____ of stress in your life.

Learn how to _____ stress in our easy _____

class. Learn techniques for deep _____ and thinking positive

thoughts. Just ten minutes each day can help you _____ and relax.

Learn to reduce _____ . You'll enjoy life more!

Classes start January 15. Call (304) 555-5689 to find out more.

C Answer the questions. Use the information from Exercise B.

1. Who is this class for? People who <u>*feel stressed out*</u> .

2. What are two symptoms of stress? You can't _____ and you _____

_____ .

3. What are two techniques you learn in the class? _____ and positive

_____ .

4. What can meditation help you to do? _____ down and _____ .

5. Do you want to take this class? Why or why not? _____

_____

A Circle the correct words.

1. The deadline is next week. You **have to** / **don't have to** register today.

2. Tomorrow is a holiday. We **have to** / **don't have to** go to school.

3. Lisa starts work at 5:00 a.m. She **has to** / **doesn't have to** wake up early.

4. Tony and Maria need a new car. They **have to** / **don't have to** save money.

5. Ramona cooked a lot of food yesterday. She **has to** / **doesn't have to** cook today.

6. I have a bad headache. I **have to** / **don't have to** take some aspirin.

B Circle the correct words.

1. **A** I feel stressed out.

   B You **ought to** / **shouldn't** do some meditation.

2. **A** I have a backache.

   B You **ought to** / **shouldn't** see a doctor.

3. **A** I feel tired and sleepy all day.

   B You **ought to** / **shouldn't** go to bed so late.

4. **A** I have too many bills.

   B You **ought to** / **shouldn't** spend so much money.

5. **A** I don't have any friends.

   B You **ought to** / **shouldn't** meet new people.

6. **A** I can't sleep at night.

   B You **ought to** / **shouldn't** drink coffee.

C Correct the mistake in each sentence. Each mistake is <u>underlined</u>.

1. George <u>don't</u> have to take the test today.
   doesn't

2. We <u>has</u> to learn how to relax.

3. Danny and Ming ought _____ register for school tomorrow.

4. Emiko shouldn't <u>to</u> get so stressed out at work.

5. Terry and Linda <u>doesn't</u> have to buy a new car this year.

6. I should <u>to</u> learn how to drive a car.

D Read the health problem. Write advice.

Problem: I have headaches all the time.

You ought to _____ .

A Complete the sentences. Use the correct form of *have to*.

1. The deadline is next week. You _*don't have to*_ register today.

2. Tomorrow is a holiday. We _____ go to school.

3. Lisa starts work at 5:00 a.m. She _____ wake up early.

4. Tony and Maria need a new car. They _____ save money.

5. Ramona cooked a lot of food yesterday. She _____ cook today.

6. I have a bad headache. I _____ take some aspirin.

B Complete the conversations.

a. spend so much money	d. drink coffee
b. do some meditation	e. see a doctor
c. go to bed so late	f. meet new people

1. **A** I feel stressed out.

   B You ought to _b_ .

2. **A** I have a backache.

   B You ought to ____ .

3. **A** I feel tired and sleepy all day.

   B You shouldn't ____ .

4. **A** I have too many bills.

   B You shouldn't ____ .

5. **A** I don't have any friends.

   B You ought to ____ .

6. **A** I can't sleep at night.

   B You shouldn't ____ .

C Correct the mistake in each sentence. Use the hint to help you.

        doesn't
1. George ~~don't~~ have to take the test today. (verb)

2. We has to learn how to relax. (verb)

3. Danny and Ming ought register for school tomorrow. (missing word)

4. Emiko shouldn't to get so stressed out at work. (extra word)

5. Terry and Linda doesn't have to buy a new car this year. (verb)

6. I should to learn how to drive a car. (extra word)

D Write a health problem. Write advice for the problem.

Problem	Advice (ought to / have to / shouldn't)

A Complete the sentences. Use the correct form of *have to* and a verb from the box.

cook	get up	go	register	save	take

1. The deadline is next week. You _*don't have to register*_ today.

2. Tomorrow is a holiday. We _____ to school.

3. Lisa starts work at 5:00 a.m. She _____ early.

4. Tony and Maria need a new car. They _____ money.

5. Ramona cooked a lot of food yesterday. She _____ today.

6. I have a bad headache. I _____ some aspirin.

B Complete the conversations. Use *ought to* or *shouldn't*.

1. **A** I feel stressed out.

   B You ___*ought to*___ do some meditation.

2. **A** I have a backache.

   B You _____ see a doctor.

3. **A** I feel tired and sleepy all day.

   B You _____ go to bed so late.

4. **A** I have too many bills.

   B You _____ spend so much money.

5. **A** I don't have any friends.

   B You _____ meet new people.

6. **A** I can't sleep at night.

   B You _____ drink coffee.

C Correct the mistake in each sentence.

1. George ~~don't~~ *doesn't* have to take the test today.

2. We has to learn how to relax.

3. Danny and Ming ought register for school tomorrow.

4. Emiko shouldn't to get so stressed out at work.

5. Terry and Linda doesn't have to buy a new car this year.

6. I should to learn how to drive a car.

D Write two health problems. Write advice for each problem.

Problem	Advice (ought to / have to / shouldn't)

Lesson C Modals

A Alan went to a job interview, but he made some mistakes. Complete the sentences. Use *should have* or *shouldn't have.*

1. He overslept. He _____ *shouldn't have* _____ stayed up so late.

2. He skipped breakfast. He _____ eaten breakfast.

3. He drove, but there was traffic. He _____ taken the bus.

4. He forgot his ID. He _____ remembered his ID.

5. He forgot his resume. He _____ forgotten his resume.

6. He didn't bring all his papers. He _____ brought all his papers.

B Naomi lost her job. Write sentences about what she should have done.

1. Naomi was always late for work.

   She should have *gotten up earlier* _____ .
   _____ (get up earlier)

2. She didn't understand her work.

   She should have _____ .
   _____ (ask questions)

3. Her co-workers didn't like her.

   She should have _____ .
   _____ (talk to her co-workers)

4. She always wore jeans.

   She should have _____ .
   _____ (wear a suit)

5. She felt nervous and stressed.

   She should have _____ .
   _____ (do some meditation)

C Write a regret you have about the past. Then give yourself advice about the past.

Regret about the past	Advice about the past
I spent last weekend by myself.	I should have called my friends.

Lesson C Modals

Name: _____

A Alan went to a job interview, but he made some mistakes. Complete the sentences. Use *should* or *shouldn't* and the verb in parentheses.

1. He overslept. He __*shouldn't*__ have __*stayed up*__ so late. (stay up)

2. He skipped breakfast. He _____ have _____ breakfast. (eat)

3. He drove, but there was traffic. He _____ have _____ the bus. (take)

4. He forgot his ID. He _____ have _____ his ID. (remember)

5. He forgot his resume. He _____ have _____ his resume. (forget)

6. He didn't bring all his papers. He _____ have _____ all his papers. (bring)

B Naomi lost her job. Write sentences about what she should have done.

asked questions	gotten up earlier	worn a suit
done some meditation	talked to her co-workers	

1. Naomi was always late for work.

   She should have gotten up earlier. _____

2. She didn't understand her work.

   _____

3. Her co-workers didn't like her.

   _____

4. She always wore jeans.

   _____

5. She felt nervous and stressed.

   _____

C Write two regrets you have about the past. Then give yourself advice about the past.

Regret about the past	Advice about the past
I spent last weekend by myself.	I should have called my friends.

Lesson C Modals

A Alan went to a job interview, but he made some mistakes. Write sentences using *should have* or *shouldn't have* and the verb in parentheses.

1. He overslept. He _shouldn't have stayed up_ so late.
    (stay up)

2. He skipped breakfast. He _____ breakfast.
    (eat)

3. He drove, but there was traffic. He _____ the bus.
    (take)

4. He forgot his ID. He _____ his ID.
    (remember)

5. He forgot his resume. He _____ his resume.
    (forget)

6. He didn't bring all his papers. He _____ all his papers.
    (bring)

B Naomi lost her job. Write sentences about what she should have done.

ask questions	get up earlier	wear a suit
do some meditation	talk to her co-workers	

1. Naomi was always late for work.

    She should have gotten up earlier.

2. She didn't understand her work.

    _____

3. Her co-workers didn't like her.

    _____

4. She always wore jeans.

    _____

5. She felt nervous and stressed.

    _____

C Write three regrets you have about the past. Then give yourself advice about the past.

Regret about the past	Advice about the past
I spent last weekend by myself.	I should have called my friends.

Lesson D Reading

A Skim the article. Find the words in *italics*. Then circle the correct part of speech for each word.

1. stressful   (adjective) / adverb
2. reaction   verb / noun
3. regularly   adjective / adverb
4. nervousness   adverb / noun
5. loosen   verb / noun

B Read the article. Match the questions and answers.

Fear OF PUBLIC SPEAKING

Speaking in public is *stressful* for everyone. It's easy to talk to a group of friends, but when you have to face a group of strangers, your knees start to shake, your throat feels dry, and you forget what you want to say. Here are some suggestions to manage the fear of public speaking.

Public speaking does not have to be stressful. It is only our *reaction* to it that causes stress. We become afraid because we think we have to be perfect every time. Speaking in public *regularly* will help reduce anxiety and *nervousness*.

What can you do to stop feeling nervous? Practice your speech in front of a mirror or in front of friends. It will help you to be well prepared, and you will feel more confident. What can you do to *loosen* tight shoulder muscles? One great tip is to breathe deeply just before you start speaking. This relaxes your body and clears your mind. Before you begin to speak, take three breaths and count to ten. That way you can stay calm when you start speaking.

---

1. What are some symptoms of stress when speaking in public? _d_

2. Why do we feel afraid of speaking in public? _____

3. Why is it a good idea to practice in front of a mirror? _____

4. Why is it a good idea to breathe deeply? _____

5. What is the main idea of the article? _____

a. It will relax your body and clear your mind.

b. How to stay calm when speaking in public.

c. We think that we have to be perfect.

d. Your knees shake and your throat feels dry.

e. It will help you to be well prepared and feel more confident.

A Skim the article. Find the words in *italics*. Then circle the correct part of speech for each word.

1. stressful   (adjective) / adverb / noun
2. reaction   verb / noun / adverb
3. regularly   adjective / adverb / verb
4. nervousness   adverb / noun / adjective
5. loosen   verb / noun / adverb

B Read the article. Answer the questions.

Fear OF PUBLIC SPEAKING

Speaking in public is *stressful* for everyone. It's easy to talk to a group of friends, but when you have to face a group of strangers, your knees start to shake, your throat feels dry, and you forget what you want to say. Here are some suggestions to manage the fear of public speaking.

Public speaking does not have to be stressful. It is only our *reaction* to it that causes stress. We become afraid because we think we have to be perfect every time. Speaking in public *regularly* will help reduce anxiety and *nervousness*.

What can you do to stop feeling nervous? Practice your speech in front of a mirror or in front of friends. It will help you to be well prepared, and you will feel more confident. What can you do to *loosen* tight shoulder muscles? One great tip is to breathe deeply just before you start speaking. This relaxes your body and clears your mind. Before you begin to speak, take three breaths and count to ten. That way you can stay calm when you start speaking.

---

1. What are some symptoms of stress when speaking in public?

   Your _____*knees*_____ shake and your throat _____*feels dry*_____ .

2. Why do we feel afraid of speaking in public?

   We think that we _____ perfect.

3. Why is it a good idea to practice in front of a mirror?

   It will help you to be _____ and feel _____ .

4. Why is it a good idea to breathe deeply?

   It will _____ your body and _____ your mind.

5. What is the main idea of the article?

   How to _____ when speaking in public.

A Skim the article. Find the words in *italics*. Then write the correct part of speech for each word.

1. stressful   _____*adjective*_____

2. reaction   _____

3. regularly   _____

4. nervousness   _____

5. loosen   _____

B Read the article. Answer the questions.

Fear OF PUBLIC SPEAKING

Speaking in public is *stressful* for everyone. It's easy to talk to a group of friends, but when you have to face a group of strangers, your knees start to shake, your throat feels dry, and you forget what you want to say. Here are some suggestions to manage the fear of public speaking.

Public speaking does not have to be stressful. It is only our *reaction* to it that causes stress. We become afraid because we think we have to be perfect every time. Speaking in public *regularly* will help reduce anxiety and *nervousness*.

What can you do to stop feeling nervous? Practice your speech in front of a mirror or in front of friends. It will help you to be well prepared, and you will feel more confident. What can you do to *loosen* tight shoulder muscles? One great tip is to breathe deeply just before you start speaking. This relaxes your body and clears your mind. Before you begin to speak, take three breaths and count to ten. That way you can stay calm when you start speaking.

1. What are some symptoms of stress when speaking in public?

    Your _*knees shake*_____ and _____ .

2. Why do we feel afraid of speaking in public?

    We think _____ .

3. Why is it a good idea to practice in front of a mirror?

    It will _____ and _____ .

4. Why is it a good idea to breathe deeply?

    It will _____ and _____ .

5. What is the main idea of this article?

    How to _____ .

A How do these people feel? Write the adjective that describes each picture.

| angry | anxious | depressed |

1 _____ *depressed* _____

2 _____

3 _____

B What do these people do when they feel depressed, angry, or anxious? Complete the sentences.

| listen to music | take deep breaths | talking with a friend | writing in my journal |

1. When I feel depressed, I like *talking with a friend* . This helps me to get another opinion about my problems. _____ also helps me to think about why I feel sad.

2. When I feel angry, I like to _____ and count to ten. This helps to reduce my blood pressure and stops me from saying something stupid.

3. When I feel anxious, I like to take a walk or _____ . This helps me relax and think about something different. I also like to make a plan for the next day because that helps me feel more in control of my life.

C Complete the sentences. Choose an adjective from Exercise A. Use the words in the box or your own ideas.

| eat chocolate | forget my problems | go to the movies |
| exercise | go shopping | think about something different |

When I feel _____ , I like to _____ .

This helps me to _____ .

A How do these people feel? Write the adjective that describes each picture.
Then write the noun form of each adjective.

angry	anxious	depressed

1

depressed

depression

2 Library CLOSED

_____

_____

3 BILL

_____

_____

B What do these people do when they feel depressed, angry, or anxious?
Complete the sentences.

count to ten	make a plan for the next day	talking with a friend
listen to music	take deep breaths	writing in my journal

1. When I feel depressed, I like *talking with a friend* _____ . This helps me
to get another opinion about my problems. _____ also
helps me to think about why I feel sad.

2. When I feel angry, I like to _____ and
_____ . This helps to reduce my blood pressure and
stops me from saying something stupid.

3. When I feel anxious, I like to take a walk or _____ .
This helps me relax and think about something different. I also like to
_____ because that helps me feel more in control of my life.

C Complete the sentences. Choose an adjective from Exercise A and
your own ideas.

When I feel _____ , I like to _____ and _____ .

This helps me to _____ and _____ .

Name: _____

Lesson E *Writing*

A How do these people feel? Write adjectives for the pictures. Then write the noun form of each adjective.

1

d _e p r e s s e d_
d _e p r e s s i o n_

2

a __ __ __ y
a __ __ er

3

a __ __ __ ous
a __ __ __ ety

B What do these people do when they feel depressed, angry, or anxious? Complete the sentences. Use the words in the box and the adjectives from Exercise A.

count to ten	make a plan for the next day	talking with a friend
listen to music	take deep breaths	writing in my journal

1. When I feel _____ *depressed* _____ , I like *talking with a friend* _____ .

   This helps me to get another opinion about my problems.

   _____ also helps me to think about

   why I feel sad.

2. When I feel _____ , I like to _____

   and _____ . This helps to reduce my blood pressure

   and stops me from saying something stupid.

3. When I feel _____ , I like to take a walk or

   _____ . This helps me relax and think about

   something different. I also like to _____

   because that helps me feel more in control of my life.

C Complete the sentences. Choose an adjective from Exercise A and your own ideas.

   When I feel _____ , I like to _____ and _____ .

   This helps me to _____ and _____ .

   I also like to _____ because _____

   _____ .

Name: _____

Lesson F Another view

A Look at the bar graph. Circle the answers.

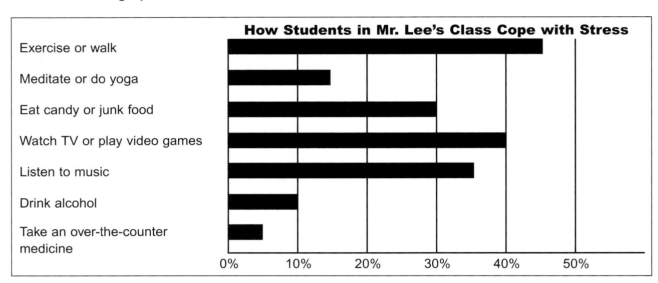

How Students in Mr. Lee's Class Cope with Stress

Exercise or walk

Meditate or do yoga

Eat candy or junk food

Watch TV or play video games

Listen to music

Drink alcohol

Take an over-the-counter medicine

0%   10%   20%   30%   40%   50%

1. This chart is about _____ .
   a. what kind of stress students have
   b. the reasons for stress
   c. how students cope with stress

2. The most popular way of managing stress was _____ .
   a. exercising or walking
   b. meditating or doing yoga
   c. eating candy or junk food

3. The least popular way of managing stress was _____ .
   a. drinking alcohol
   b. taking an over-the-counter medication
   c. exercising or walking

4. Watching TV was less popular than _____ .
   a. drinking alcohol
   b. exercising or walking
   c. taking an over-the-counter medicine

5. Meditating or doing yoga was more popular than _____ .
   a. eating candy or junk food
   b. listening to music
   c. drinking alcohol

6. Eating candy or junk food was more popular than _____ .
   a. listening to music
   b. watching TV
   c. meditating or doing yoga

B Answer the questions.

1. Which was more popular – listening to music or playing video games? _____

_____

2. Which was less popular – drinking alcohol or eating junk food? _____

3. What percentage of the students exercise to manage stress? _____

Lesson F Another view

A Look at the bar graph. Circle the answers.

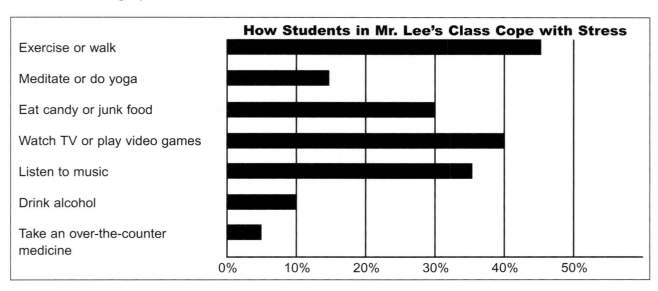

How Students in Mr. Lee's Class Cope with Stress

- Exercise or walk
- Meditate or do yoga
- Eat candy or junk food
- Watch TV or play video games
- Listen to music
- Drink alcohol
- Take an over-the-counter medicine

0% 10% 20% 30% 40% 50%

1. This chart is about _____ .
   a. what kind of stress students have
   b. the reasons for stress
   (c.) how students cope with stress
   d. how to reduce stress

2. The most popular way of managing stress was _____ .
   a. exercising or walking
   b. meditating or doing yoga
   c. eating candy or junk food
   d. listening to music

3. The least popular way of managing stress was _____ .
   a. drinking alcohol
   b. taking an over-the-counter medication
   c. exercising or walking
   d. eating candy or junk food

4. Watching TV was less popular than _____ .
   a. drinking alcohol
   b. exercising or walking
   c. taking an over-the-counter medicine
   d. listening to music

5. Meditating or doing yoga was more popular than _____ .
   a. eating candy or junk food
   b. listening to music
   c. drinking alcohol
   d. exercising or walking

6. Eating candy or junk food was more popular than _____ .
   a. listening to music
   b. watching TV
   c. meditating or doing yoga
   d. exercising or walking

B Write questions. Then write answers.

1. Which / more popular – / listening to music / playing video games / was / or

_____

2. Which / or / less popular – / drinking alcohol / was / eating junk food

_____

3. What / exercise / of the students / to manage / percentage / stress

_____

Name: _____

A Look at the bar graph. Answer the questions.

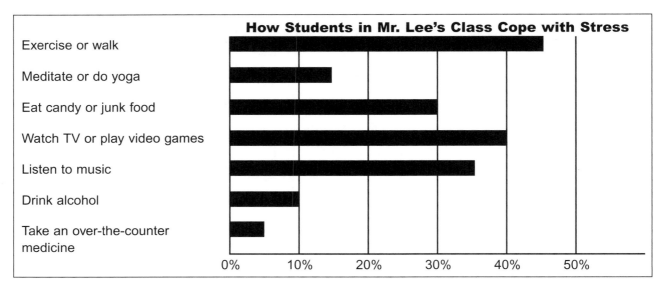

How Students in Mr. Lee's Class Cope with Stress

Exercise or walk

Meditate or do yoga

Eat candy or junk food

Watch TV or play video games

Listen to music

Drink alcohol

Take an over-the-counter medicine

0%   10%   20%   30%   40%   50%

1. What is this bar graph about? *How students cope with stress.*
2. What was the most popular way of managing stress? _____
3. What was the least popular way of managing stress? _____
4. Watching TV was less popular than which activity? _____
5. Meditating or doing yoga was more popular than which activity? _____
6. Eating candy or junk food was more popular than which activity? _____

B Write four more questions and answers about the information in the bar graph.

1. Question: _____

   Answer: _____

2. Question: _____

   Answer: _____

3. Question: _____

   Answer: _____

4. Question: _____

   Answer: _____

Lesson A Get ready

☑ ■ ■

A Circle the answers.

1. Volunteering is a very enjoyable and _____ activity.
   (a.) worthwhile   b. patient

2. Pat organizes volunteer programs. She is the volunteer _____ .
   a. resident   b. coordinator

3. To find out more about volunteering, come to the _____ .
   a. commitment   b. orientation

4. Francisco is very calm and doesn't get angry. He's very _____ .
   a. patient   b. worthwhile

5. You need to make a _____ of at least three hours a week.
   a. orientation   b. commitment

6. Be compassionate when you talk to _____ in our nursing home.
   a. residents   b. volunteers

B Complete the conversation. Use the answers from Exercise A.

Leo Hi, Dave. Where are you going?

Dave I'm going to my volunteer job at the local nursing home.

Leo That sounds interesting. What do you do there?

Dave I just talk to the _____*residents*_____ and keep them company. It makes them feel better.

Leo Is it difficult? I bet you have to be very _____ .

Dave It's not hard at all. And it feels good to do something _____ for other people.

Leo Do you go every week?

Dave Yes, I had to make a _____ of at least one hour a week when I started.

Leo One hour a week isn't much. Do you think I could do that, too?

Dave Sure! Why don't you come along and talk to the volunteer _____ ? Maybe you can come to the next _____ and find out more.

C What kind of volunteer work could you do in these places? Write your ideas.

Nursing home	Park
Talk to residents	

Lesson A Get ready

A Complete the sentences.

| commitment | coordinator | orientation | patient | residents | worthwhile |

1. Volunteering is a very enjoyable and _____*worthwhile*_____ activity.

2. Pat organizes volunteer programs. She is the volunteer _____ .

3. To find out more about volunteering, come to the _____ .

4. Francisco is very calm and doesn't get angry. He's very _____ .

5. You need to make a _____ of at least three hours a week.

6. Be compassionate when you talk to _____ in our nursing home.

B Complete the conversation. Use the words from Exercise A and the questions in the box.

| Do you go every week? | Is it difficult? | Where are you going? |
| Do you think I could do that, too? | What do you do there? | |

Leo Hi, Dave. *Where are you going?* _____

Dave I'm going to my volunteer job at the local nursing home.

Leo That sounds interesting. _____

Dave I just talk to the _____*residents*_____ and keep them company. It makes them

feel better.

Leo _____ I bet you have to be very _____ .

Dave It's not hard at all. And it feels good to do something _____

for other people.

Leo _____

Dave Yes, I had to make a _____ of at least one hour a week

when I started.

Leo One hour a week isn't much. _____

Dave Sure! Why don't you come along and talk to the volunteer _____ ?

Maybe you can come to the next _____ and find out more.

C What kind of volunteer work could you do in these places? Write your ideas.
Use the back of this paper.

| hospital | nursing home | park |

Lesson A Get ready

■ ■ ☑

A Complete the sentences.

1. Volunteering is a very enjoyable and w _o_ _r_ _t_ _h_ _w_ _h_ _i_ _l_ e activity.

2. Pat organizes volunteer programs. She is the volunteer

   c _ _ _ _ _ _ _ _ r.

3. To find out more about volunteering, come to the

   o _ _ _ _ _ _ _ _ _ n.

4. Francisco is very calm and doesn't get angry. He's very p _ _ _ _ _ t.

5. You need to make a c _ _ _ _ _ _ _ _ t
   of at least three hours a week.

6. Be compassionate when you talk to r _ _ _ _ _ _ _ s
   in our nursing home.

B Complete the conversation. Use the words from Exercise A. Then number the sentences in the correct order.

_1_ **Leo** Hi, Dave. Where are you going?

____ **Leo** That sounds interesting. What do you do there?

____ **Dave** It's not hard at all. And it feels good to do something _____ for

   other people.

____ **Leo** Do you go every week?

____ **Leo** Is it difficult? I bet you have to be very _____ .

____ **Dave** I'm going to my volunteer job at the local nursing home.

____ **Leo** One hour a week isn't much. Do you think I could do that, too?

____ **Dave** Yes, I had to make a _____ of at least one hour a week

   when I started.

_10_ **Dave** Sure! Why don't you come along and talk to the volunteer

   _____ ? Maybe you can come to the next

   _____ and find out more.

____ **Dave** I just talk to the _____ and keep them company.

   It makes them feel better.

C What kind of volunteer work could you do in these places? Write your ideas.
Use the back of this paper.

| hospital | nursing home | park | school |

Name: _____

Lesson B Time clauses

A Circle the correct words.

1. (As soon as) / **Until** I finish lunch, I'll take my medication.

2. Tina will work in the garden **as soon as** / **until** it gets dark.

3. Adina will have her birthday lunch **as soon as** / **until** her family arrives.

4. **As soon as** / **Until** I feel stronger, I'll start exercising again.

5. We will stay with you **as soon as** / **until** visitors have to leave.

6. Stan and Frank will play cards **as soon as** / **until** it is time for dinner.

B Robert and Rosalita are going to attend volunteer training tomorrow. Read their schedule. Match.

Volunteer Training: Schedule of Activities

- **Welcome breakfast** (coffee and muffins): 9:00 a.m.–9:30 a.m.
- **Orientation and self-introductions**: 9:30 a.m.–10:00 a.m.
- **Internet and computer skills**: 10:00 a.m.–noon
- **Lunch break / free Internet access**: noon–1:00 p.m.
- **Team activities** (volleyball, baseball, or table tennis): 1:00 p.m.–3:00 p.m.

---

1. As soon as they arrive, _c_

2. They'll have an orientation _____

3. They'll listen to introductions _____

4. As soon as they finish the computer-skills class, _____

5. They'll use the Internet _____

6. They'll play sports with other volunteers _____

a. until lunch break is over.

b. they'll have lunch.

c. they'll have breakfast.

d. until the computer-skills class starts.

e. as soon as lunch break is over.

f. as soon as they finish breakfast.

C What will you do today? Complete the sentences with information about yourself.

1. As soon as I finish class, I'll _____ .

2. I'll _____ as soon as I get home.

3. I'll _____ until I go to bed.

A Complete the sentences. Use *as soon as* or *until*.

1. _As soon as_____ I finish lunch, I'll take my medication.

2. Tina will work in the garden _____ it gets dark.

3. Adina will have her birthday lunch _____ her family arrives.

4. _____ I feel stronger, I'll start exercising again.

5. We will stay with you _____ visitors have to leave.

6. Stan and Frank will play cards _____ it is time for dinner.

B Robert and Rosalita are going to attend volunteer training tomorrow. Read their schedule. Complete the sentences with *as soon as* or *until*.

> ## Volunteer Training: Schedule of Activities
>
> - **Welcome breakfast** (coffee and muffins): 9:00 a.m.–9:30 a.m.
> - **Orientation and self-introductions**: 9:30 a.m.–10:00 a.m.
> - **Internet and computer skills**: 10:00 a.m.–noon
> - **Lunch break / free Internet access**: noon–1:00 p.m.
> - **Team activities** (volleyball, baseball, or table tennis): 1:00 p.m.–3:00 p.m.

1. _As soon as_____ they arrive, they'll have breakfast.

2. They'll have an orientation _____ they finish breakfast.

3. They'll listen to introductions _____ the computer-skills class starts.

4. _____ they finish the computer-skills class, they'll have lunch.

5. They'll use the Internet _____ lunch break is over.

6. They'll play sports with other volunteers _____ lunch break is over.

C What will you do today? Complete the sentences with information about yourself.

1. As soon as I finish class, I'll _____ .

2. I'll _____ as soon as I get home.

3. Until it's time for dinner, I'll _____ .

4. I'll _____ until I go to bed.

Lesson B Time clauses

A Complete the sentences. Circle the correct time clause and use a verb from the box.

have	play	start	stay	take	work

1. (As soon as) / **Until** I finish lunch, I'll _____*take*_____ my medication.

2. Tina will _____ in the garden **as soon as** / **until** it gets dark.

3. Adina will _____ her birthday lunch **as soon as** / **until** her family arrives.

4. **As soon as** / **Until** I feel stronger, I'll _____ exercising again.

5. We will _____ with you **as soon as** / **until** visitors have to leave.

6. Stan and Frank will _____ cards **as soon as** / **until** it is time for dinner.

B Robert and Rosalita are going to attend volunteer training tomorrow. Read their schedule. Write sentences with *as soon as* or *until*.

Volunteer Training: Schedule of Activities

- **Welcome breakfast** (coffee and muffins): 9:00 a.m.–9:30 a.m.
- **Orientation and self-introductions**: 9:30 a.m.–10:00 a.m.
- **Internet and computer skills**: 10:00 a.m.–noon
- **Lunch break / free Internet access**: noon–1:00 p.m.
- **Team activities** (volleyball, baseball, or table tennis): 1:00 p.m.–3:00 p.m.

---

1. arrive / have breakfast
   *As soon as they arrive, they'll have breakfast.*_____

2. have an orientation / finish breakfast
   _____

3. listen to introductions / computer-skills class starts
   _____

4. finish the computer-skills class / have lunch
   _____

5. use the Internet / lunch break is over
   _____

6. play sports with other volunteers / lunch break is over
   _____

C What will you do today? Write two sentences with *as soon as* and two sentences with *until*. Use the back of this paper.

Lesson C *Verb tense contrast*

☑■■

A Match the time expressions.

1. on Thursdays __b__
2. in January and July _____
3. in January, March, and July _____
4. on Monday and Wednesday _____
5. on the 1st and the 15th of each month _____
6. on Monday, Wednesday, and Friday _____

a. twice a week
b. once a week
c. twice a month
d. twice a year
e. three times a year
f. three times a week

B Circle the correct form of the verbs.

1. We **visit** / **visited** / **have visited** children in the hospital 12 times last year.

2. We **take** / **took** / **have taken** seniors on trips six times so far this year.

3. We **cook** / **cooked** / **have cooked** meals for homeless people once a week.

4. We **clean up** / **cleaned up** / **have cleaned up** local parks five times last year.

5. We **do** / **did** / **have done** volunteer training twice a month.

6. We **collect** / **collected** / **have collected** money for poor people many times so far this year.

C Correct the mistake in each sentence. Each mistake is <u>underlined</u>.

1. Adam <u>~~take~~</u> *took* his neighbor to the doctor every week last year.

2. Flavia <u>have</u> delivered toys to children three times so far this year.

3. Anna and Gino <u>reads</u> stories to children in the hospital once a month.

4. I <u>has</u> volunteered at the homeless shelter many times.

5. How often have you <u>volunteer</u> so far this year?

6. How many times <u>have</u> you volunteer last year?

D How often have you helped a family member so far this year? What did you do?

Example: *I have helped a family member three times so far this year. For example,*

I helped my cousin clean up his yard.

_____

_____

Name: _____

Lesson C Verb tense contrast

A Complete the time expressions. Use *once*, *twice*, or *three times*.

1. on Thursdays   _____once_____ a week

2. in January and July   _____ a year

3. in January, March, and July   _____ a year

4. on Monday and Wednesday   _____ a week

5. on the 1st and the 15th of each month   _____ a month

6. on Monday, Wednesday, and Friday   _____ a week

B Complete the sentences. Use the present, present perfect, or past form of the verbs in parentheses.

1. We _____*visited*_____ children in the hospital 12 times last year.
   (visit)

2. We _____ seniors on trips six times so far this year.
   (take)

3. We _____ meals for homeless people once a week.
   (cook)

4. We _____ local parks five times last year.
   (clean up)

5. We _____ volunteer training twice a month.
   (do)

6. We _____ money for poor people many times so far this year.
   (collect)

C Correct the mistake in each sentence.

1. Adam ~~take~~ *took* his neighbor to the doctor every week last year.

2. Flavia have delivered toys to children three times so far this year.

3. Anna and Gino reads stories to children in the hospital once a month.

4. I has volunteered at the homeless shelter many times.

5. How often have you volunteer so far this year?

6. How many times you volunteer last year?

D How often have you helped a family member or neighbor so far this year? What did you do? Give two examples.

Example: *I have helped a family member three times so far this year. For example,*

I helped my cousin clean up his yard. . . .

_____

_____

_____

Lesson C *Verb tenses* ■■☑

A Write time expressions that mean the same. Use words from each box.

once	twice	three times		a week	a month	a year

1. on Thursdays   _____*once a week*_____

2. in January and July   _____

3. in January, March, and July   _____

4. on Monday and Wednesday   _____

5. on the 1st and the 15th of each month   _____

6. on Monday, Wednesday, and Friday   _____

B Complete the sentences. Use the present, present perfect, or past form of the verbs.

clean up	collect	cook	do	take	visit

1. We _____*visited*_____ children in the hospital 12 times last year.

2. We _____ seniors on trips six times so far this year.

3. We _____ meals for homeless people once a week.

4. We _____ up local parks five times last year.

5. We _____ volunteer training twice a month.

6. We _____ money for poor people many times so far this year.

C Correct the mistakes. There are two mistakes in each sentence.
1. Adam ~~take~~ *took* his neighbor to the doctor every week~~s~~ last year.

2. Flavia have delivered toys to children three time so far this year.

3. Anna and Gino reads stories to children in the hospital once month.

4. I has volunteered at the homeless shelter many time.

5. How often you have volunteer so far this year?

6. How many times you volunteered last year?

D How often have you helped a family member or neighbor so far this year?
What did you do? Write three examples on the back of this paper.

Example: *I have helped a family member three times so far this year. For example,*

I helped my cousin clean up his yard. . . .

Lesson D Reading

A Skim the article. Find the words in *italics*. Then circle the correct definition for each word.

1. insecure	a. friendly	(b.) not confident
2. grave	a. serious	b. common
3. impaired	a. damaged	b. assisted
4. tenacity	a. weakness	b. strength
5. gratifying	a. funny	b. satisfying
6. rewarding	a. fun	b. valuable

B Read the article. Match the questions and the answers.

A WORTHWHILE **COMMITMENT**

Big Brothers is an organization that connects young people with caring adults. Just one hour a week of your time and attention can help a child or a teenager become confident and successful. You can make a difference!

When Rick met 14-year-old Leon, he remembered how much he needed a friend when he was that age. Leon was lonely and *insecure*. He had no hearing in one ear because of a *grave* illness when he was a baby. Rick began meeting Leon once a week, and now they are good friends.

"You have to make a commitment," says Rick, "but you can share the kinds of activities you already like to do, such as eating pizza or playing sports." Together they talk about being hearing-*impaired* and coping with problems at school. "I admire his *tenacity*," says Rick. "He doesn't give up. It's *gratifying* to feel that he trusts me. I feel like a better person. I'm helping him, but he helps me a lot, too."

Rick recommends the experience. "Being a Big Brother is fun and worthwhile," says Rick. "I've learned so much. It's the most *rewarding* thing I have ever done."

1. What do people from Big Brothers do? __b__

2. How often does Rick meet with Leon? _____

3. What was Leon like at first? _____

4. What does Rick admire about Leon? _____

5. What is the main idea of the article? _____

a. He admires his tenacity.

b. They help young people become confident.

c. They meet once a week.

d. Volunteering is fun and worthwhile.

e. He was lonely and insecure.

C Internet task: Go on the Internet. Find a volunteer organization. Write the information. If you do not have access to the Internet, write about an organization you know.

Name of organization: _____

Main activity: _____

Lesson D Reading

■ ☑ ■

A Skim the article. Find the words in *italics*. Then match each word with the correct definition.

1. insecure _b_   a. serious

2. grave _____   b. not confident

3. impaired _____   c. satisfying

4. tenacity _____   d. valuable

5. gratifying _____   e. damaged

6. rewarding _____   f. strength

B Read the article. Answer the questions.

A WORTHWHILE **COMMITMENT**

Big Brothers is an organization that connects young people with caring adults. Just one hour a week of your time and attention can help a child or a teenager become confident and successful. You can make a difference!

When Rick met 14-year-old Leon, he remembered how much he needed a friend when he was that age. Leon was lonely and *insecure*. He had no hearing in one ear because of a *grave* illness when he was a baby. Rick began meeting Leon once a week, and now they are good friends.

"You have to make a commitment," says Rick, "but you can share the kinds of activities you already like to do, such as eating pizza or playing sports." Together they talk about being hearing-*impaired* and coping with problems at school. "I admire his *tenacity*," says Rick. "He doesn't give up. It's *gratifying* to feel that he trusts me. I feel like a better person. I'm helping him, but he helps me a lot, too."

Rick recommends the experience. "Being a Big Brother is fun and worthwhile," says Rick. "I've learned so much. It's the most *rewarding* thing I have ever done."

1. What do people from Big Brothers do? They help young people become _____*confident*_____ .

2. How often does Rick meet with Leon? They meet _____ .

3. What was Leon like at first? He was _____ and _____ .

4. What does Rick admire about Leon? He admires _____ .

5. What is the main idea of the article? Volunteering is _____ and _____ .

C Internet task: Go on the Internet. Find two volunteer organizations. Write the information. If you do not have access to the Internet, write about organizations you know. Use the back of this paper.

Name of organization: _____   Main activity: _____

Lesson D *Reading*

■ ■ ☑

A Skim the article. Find the words in *italics*. Then write them next to their definitions.

1. _____*insecure*_____ : not confident

2. _____ : serious

3. _____ : damaged

4. _____ : strength

5. _____ : satisfying

6. _____ : valuable

B Read the article. Answer the questions.

A WORTHWHILE **COMMITMENT**

Big Brothers is an organization that connects young people with caring adults. Just one hour a week of your time and attention can help a child or a teenager become confident and successful. You can make a difference!

When Rick met 14-year-old Leon, he remembered how much he needed a friend when he was that age. Leon was lonely and *insecure*. He had no hearing in one ear because of a *grave* illness when he was a baby. Rick began meeting Leon once a week, and now they are good friends.

"You have to make a commitment," says Rick, "but you can share the kinds of activities you already like to do, such as eating pizza or playing sports." Together they talk about being hearing-*impaired* and coping with problems at school. "I admire his *tenacity*," says Rick. "He doesn't give up. It's *gratifying* to feel that he trusts me. I feel like a better person. I'm helping him, but he helps me a lot, too."

Rick recommends the experience. "Being a Big Brother is fun and worthwhile," says Rick. "I've learned so much. It's the most *rewarding* thing I have ever done."

1. What do people from Big Brothers do? They help young *people become confident* .

2. How often does Rick meet with Leon? They _____ .

3. What was Leon like at first? He was _____ .

4. What does Rick admire about Leon? He _____ .

5. What is the main idea of the article? Volunteering is _____ .

C Internet task: Go on the Internet. Find three volunteer organizations. Write the information on a separate piece of paper. If you do not have access to the Internet, write about organizations you know.

Name of organization: _____   Main activity: _____

A Complete the sentences.

As soon as	eye doctors	Last year
difference	help other people	

My brother, Andrew, and his wife, Lucy, are two of the most caring people I have ever met. They are _____ *eye doctors* _____ , and they have an eye clinic in Kansas City. Every year, they do something worthwhile to _____ . When patients come to the clinic to get new glasses, Andrew and Lucy ask them to donate their old glasses. _____ , they collected several hundred pairs of glasses. Then they spent two weeks working in a hospital in Calcutta, India. _____ they arrived, people started to make a line in front of the hospital. Six hundred people got a free eye test and a free pair of glasses. It made a huge _____ in their lives.

B Match questions and answers. Use the information from Exercise A.

1. **Who** made a difference? _c_
2. **What** did they do? ____
3. **Why** did they do it? ____
4. **Where** did this happen? ____
5. **When** did it happen? ____
6. **How** did they make a difference? ____

a. Collected old glasses and gave them away.
b. In Kansas City and Calcutta, India.
c. Andrew and Lucy.
d. Last year.
e. Six hundred people got a free eye test and a free pair of glasses.
f. To help other people.

C Think of a teacher you know who made a difference. Complete the chart. Then work with a partner. Ask your partner the questions.

Questions	Answers
Who made a difference?	
What did this person do?	
Why did this person do it?	
Where did this happen?	
When did it happen?	
How did this person make a difference?	

Lesson E Writing

A Complete the sentences.

As soon as	difference	help other people	worthwhile
caring	eye doctors	Last year	

My brother, Andrew, and his wife, Lucy, are two of the most ___caring___ people

I have ever met. They are _____ , and they have an eye clinic in Kansas City.

Every year, they do something _____ to _____ . When patients come

to the clinic to get new glasses, Andrew and Lucy ask them to donate their old glasses.

_____ , they collected several hundred pairs of glasses. Then they spent two

weeks working in a hospital in Calcutta, India. _____ they arrived, people

started to make a line in front of the hospital. Six hundred people got a free eye test

and a free pair of glasses. It made a huge _____ in their lives.

B Answer the questions. Use the information from Exercise A.

1. **Who** made a difference?   ___Andrew___ and ___Lucy___ .

2. **What** did they do?   _____ old glasses and _____ them away.

3. **Why** did they do it?   To _____ .

4. **Where** did this happen?   In _____ and _____ .

5. **When** did it happen?   Last _____ .

6. **How** did they make a difference?   Six hundred people _____

   _____ .

C Think of a teacher you know who made a difference. Complete the chart. Then work
with a partner. Ask your partner the questions.

Questions	Answers
Who made a difference?	
What did this person do?	
Why did this person do it?	
Where did this happen?	
When did it happen?	
How did this person make a difference?	

Lesson E Writing

■ ■ ☑

A Complete the sentences.

As soon as	difference	help other people	met	worthwhile
caring	eye doctors	Last year	patients	

My brother, Andrew, and his wife, Lucy, are two of the most

_____*caring*_____ people I have ever _____ . They are

_____ , and they have an eye clinic in Kansas City. Every year,

they do something _____ to _____ .

When _____ come to the clinic to get new glasses, Andrew and Lucy

ask them to donate their old glasses. _____ , they collected several

hundred pairs of glasses. Then they spent two weeks working in a hospital in

Calcutta, India. _____ they arrived, people started to make a line

in front of the hospital. Six hundred people got a free eye test and a free pair of

glasses. It made a huge _____ in their lives.

B Complete the questions. Then complete the chart. Use the information from Exercise A.

How	What	When	Where	Who	Why

Questions	Answers
1. _____*Who*_____ made a difference?	Andrew *and Lucy* _____ .
2. _____ did they do?	Collected _____ .
3. _____ did they do it?	To _____ .
4. _____ did this happen?	In _____ .
5. _____ did it happen?	Last _____ .
6. _____ did they make a difference?	_____ .

C Think of a teacher you know who made a difference. Write a paragraph on a separate piece of paper. Include details that answer all the *Wh-* questions. Then share your paragraph with a partner.

Name: _____

A Read the ad. Then circle the answers.

Hospital Volunteer Opportunities

To participate as a volunteer, you must be at least 16 years old and make a commitment of three hours a week for six months. Attendance at one 3-hour orientation session is required. **No experience is necessary.**

  Volunteers will:
  • Deliver toys and games to sick children
  • Read stories and play games with children
  • Greet visitors and serve water and soft drinks

1. How old do you need to be?
   a. 18 years old   (b.) at least 16 years old

2. What time commitment is required?
   a. three hours a week for a year   b. three hours a week for six months

3. What kind of training is required?
   a. an orientation session   b. none

4. What kind of experience is needed?
   a. working with children   b. none

5. What are some of the job duties?
   a. delivering toys, reading stories, greeting visitors   b. tutoring children

B Circle the correct words to make popular sayings about giving.

1. From small beginnings come **better** / (**great**) things.

2. Many hands make **great** / **light** work.

3. The best things in life are **free** / **great**.

4 It's **better** / **great** to give than to receive.

C Internet task: Go on the Internet. Find a volunteer opportunity in your town. Write the information. If you do not have access to the Internet, write about a volunteer opportunity you know.

Organization	Time commitment	Duties

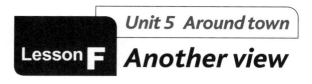

A Read the ad. Then match the questions with the answers.

Hospital Volunteer Opportunities

To participate as a volunteer, you must be at least 16 years old and make a commitment of three hours a week for six months. Attendance at one 3-hour orientation session is required. **No experience is necessary.**

  Volunteers will:
  • Deliver toys and games to sick children
  • Read stories and play games with children
  • Greet visitors and serve water and soft drinks

1. How old do you need to be? _*b*_

2. What time commitment is required? ____

3. What kind of training is required? ____

4. What kind of experience is needed? ____

5. What are some of the job duties? ____

a. You don't need any experience.

b. You need to be at least 16 years old.

c. You need to attend an orientation session.

d. You need to work 3 hours a week for six months.

e. Delivering toys, reading stories, and greeting visitors.

B Complete these popular sayings about giving.

better	free	great	light

1. From small beginnings come _____*great*_____ things.

2. Many hands make _____ work.

3. The best things in life are _____ .

4. It's _____ to give than to receive.

C Internet task: Go on the Internet. Find two volunteer opportunities in your town. Write the information. If you do not have access to the Internet, write about volunteer opportunities you know.

Organization	Time commitment	Duties	

Lesson F Another view

A Read the ad. Then answer the questions.

Hospital Volunteer Opportunities

To participate as a volunteer, you must be at least 16 years old and make a commitment of three hours a week for six months. Attendance at one 3-hour orientation session is required. **No experience is necessary.**

Volunteers will:
- Deliver toys and games to sick children
- Read stories and play games with children
- Greet visitors and serve water and soft drinks

1. How old do you need to be?

   You need to be _at least 16 years old._____

2. What time commitment is required?

   You need to work _____

3. What kind of training is required?

   You need to _____

4. What kind of experience is needed?

   You don't need _____

5. What are some of the job duties?

   _____

B Complete the popular sayings about giving.

1. From small beginnings come _____great_____ things.

2. Many hands make _____ work.

3. The best things in life are _____ .

4. It's _____ to give than to receive.

C Internet task: Go on the Internet. Find three volunteer opportunities in your town. Write the information. If you do not have access to the Internet, write about volunteer opportunities you know.

Organization	Time commitment	Duties

Name: _____

☑ ■ ■

A Circle the answers.

1. A DVD player is an _____ device that plays DVDs.
   a. manual   (b.) electronic

2. People shouldn't use their cell phones in the library. It's _____ .
   a. distracting   b. convenient

3. When you find a new way of doing something, it is _____ .
   a. electronic   b. innovative

4. I get too much _____ in my e-mail, and it takes time to delete it.
   a. text   b. spam

5. I think cell phones are useful and save time. They're very _____ .
   a. interesting   b. convenient

6. You can send _____ on a cell phone.
   a. devices   b. text messages

B Complete the sentences. Use *saves* or *wastes*.

1. A cell phone __*saves*__ time because you don't need to look for a pay phone.

2. E-mail _____ time because you have to delete lots of spam.

3. A calculator _____ time because you don't have to do math in your head.

4. A digital camera _____ time because you take too many pictures.

5. Using a computer _____ time because it's faster than writing by hand.

6. The Internet _____ time because you don't need to go to the library.

C Write the names of your two favorite time-saving devices. Then write your opinion about whether the devices save or waste time. If you don't know the name of a device in English, draw a picture of it.

Device	Your opinion

Lesson A *Get ready*

Name: _____

A Complete the sentences.

convenient	distracting	electronic	innovative	spam	text messages

1. A DVD player is an _____ *electronic* _____ device that plays DVDs.

2. People shouldn't use their cell phones in the library. It's _____ .

3. When you find a new way of doing something, it is _____ .

4. I get too much _____ in my e-mail, and it takes time to delete it.

5. I think cell phones are useful and save time. They're very _____ .

6. You can send _____ on a cell phone.

B Complete the sentences. Use the words in the box.

calculator	cell phone	computer	digital camera	e-mail	the Internet

1. A _____ *cell phone* _____ saves time because you don't need to look for a pay phone.

2. _____ wastes time because you have to delete lots of spam.

3. A _____ saves time because you don't have to do math in your head.

4. A _____ wastes time because you take too many pictures.

5. Using a _____ saves time because it's faster than writing by hand.

6. _____ saves time because you don't need to go to the library.

C Write the names of your three favorite time-saving devices. Then write your opinion about whether the devices save or waste time. If you don't know the name of a device in English, draw a picture of it.

Device	Your opinion

Lesson A *Get ready*

A Complete the sentences.

1. A DVD player is an e _l_ _e_ _c_ _t_ _r_ _o_ _n_ _i_ c device that plays DVDs.

2. People shouldn't use their cell phones in the library.

   It's d__ __ __ __ __ __ __ __ __g.

3. When you find a new way of doing something, it is i__ __ __ __ __ __ __ __ve.

4. I get too much s__ __m in my e-mail, and it takes time to delete it.

5. I think cell phones are useful and save time. They're very c__ __ __ __ __ __ __ __ __t.

6. You can send t__ __t m__ __ __ __ __ __s on a cell phone.

B Complete the sentences with the phrases in the box. Use *saves* or *wastes*.

it's faster than writing by hand	you don't need to look for a pay phone
you don't need to go to the library	you have to delete lots of spam
you don't have to do math in your head	you take too many pictures

1. A cell phone ____saves____ time because ___you don't need to look for a pay phone___ .

2. E-mail _____ time because _____ .

3. A calculator _____ time because _____ .

4. A digital camera _____ time because _____ .

5. Using a computer _____ time because _____ .

6. The Internet _____ time because _____ .

C Write the names of your four favorite time-saving devices. Then write your opinion about whether the devices save or waste time. If you don't know the name of a device in English, draw a picture of it.

Device	Your opinion

Lesson B *Clauses of concession*   Name: _____

A Combine the sentences.

1. I have a cell phone. I prefer to use e-mail.

   Even though *I have a cell phone, I prefer to use e-mail* .

2. My brother lives nearby. I don't see him much.

   Even though _____ , _____ .

3. Jerry prefers to write letters by hand. He has e-mail at home.

   _____ even though _____ .

4. Steve has a car. He rides his bicycle to work every day.

   Even though _____ , _____ .

5. Wanda doesn't want an air conditioner. Her house gets hot in summer.

   _____ even though _____ .

6. Olga loves watching movies. She doesn't want a DVD player.

   Even though _____ , _____ .

B Roberta has a lot of technology in her home. Complete the sentences.

an air conditioner	a computer	a dryer
a cell phone	a dishwasher	a DVD player

1. Although she has _____ *a computer* _____ , she doesn't use the Internet at home.

2. Although she has _____ , she doesn't call me.

3. Although she has _____ , she goes to the movies a lot.

4. Although she has _____ , she hangs her washing on the line.

5. Although she has _____ , she uses a fan.

6. Although she has _____ , she washes dishes in the sink.

C Complete the sentences with information about yourself.

Example: Although I have a *DVD player at home* , I prefer to *go to the movies* .

1. Although I have a _____ , I prefer to _____ .

2. I don't like to _____ even though _____ .

94   Add Ventures 4   © Cambridge University Press 2009 **Photocopiable**

Name: _____

Lesson **B** *Clauses of concession*

A Combine the sentences. Use *even though*.

1. I have a cell phone. I prefer to use e-mail.

   Even though I have a cell phone, I prefer to use e-mail.

2. My brother lives nearby. I don't see him much.

   _____

3. Jerry prefers to write letters by hand. He has e-mail at home.

   _____

4. Steve has a car. He rides his bicycle to work every day.

   _____

5. Wanda doesn't want an air conditioner. Her house gets hot in summer.

   _____

6. Olga loves watching movies. She doesn't want a DVD player.

   _____

B Roberta has a lot of technology in her home. Complete the sentences.
Use *although*.

an air conditioner	a computer	a dryer
a cell phone	a dishwasher	a DVD player

1. *Although she has a computer* _____ , she doesn't use the Internet at home.
2. _____ , she doesn't call me.
3. _____ , she goes to the movies a lot.
4. _____ , she hangs her washing on the line.
5. _____ , she uses a fan.
6. _____ , she washes dishes in the sink.

C Complete the sentences with information about yourself.

Example: Although I have a *DVD player at home* , I prefer to *go to the movies* .

1. Although I have a _____ , I prefer to _____ .
2. I don't like to _____ even though _____ .
3. Even though _____ , I don't like to _____ .

Lesson B Clauses of concession

A Match. Then combine the sentences. Use *even though*.

1. I have a cell phone. __e__
2. My brother lives nearby. ____
3. Jerry prefers to write letters by hand. ____
4. Steve has a car. ____
5. Wanda doesn't want an air conditioner. ____
6. Olga loves watching movies. ____

a. He has e-mail at home.
b. She doesn't want a DVD player.
c. He rides his bicycle to work every day.
d. I don't see him much.
e. I prefer to use e-mail.
f. Her house gets hot in summer.

1. *Even though I have a cell phone, I prefer to use e-mail.* _____
2. _____
3. _____
4. _____
5. _____
6. _____

B Roberta has a lot of technology in her home. Complete the sentences.
Use *although*.

1. *Although she has a computer* _____ , she doesn't use the Internet at home.
2. _____ , she doesn't call me.
3. _____ , she goes to the movies a lot.
4. _____ , she hangs her washing on the line.
5. _____ , she uses a fan.
6. _____ , she washes dishes in the sink.

C Complete the sentences with information about yourself.

Example: Although I have a _DVD player at home_ , I prefer to _go to the movies_ .

1. Although I have a _____ , I prefer to _____ .
2. I don't like to _____ even though _____ .
3. Even though _____ , I don't like to _____ .
4. I always _____ although _____ .

Lesson C *Clauses of reason and concession*

A Circle the correct words.

1. **Because** / **Although** an electric oven takes longer, I prefer to cook with one.

2. **Because** / **Although** an electronic dictionary is light, Jim keeps one in his backpack.

3. **Because** / **Although** a dryer is noisy, Lucas uses one when he does laundry.

4. **Because** / **Although** dishwashers use a lot of water, we wash our dishes by hand.

5. **Because** / **Although** biking is good exercise, I bike to work.

6. **Because** / **Although** I am an excellent cook, I usually eat out.

B Correct the sentences. Add the missing word.

1. Although he has a car, Sam takes the subway to work. (he)

2. Frank talks to his friends over the Internet it is free. (because)

3. Although they save a lot of time, I like electrical appliances. (don't)

4. Victor buys his lunch because he doesn't time to make one at home. (have)

5. It is faster by subway, Joe and Mei-Lin drive to work. (although)

6. We often buy food online although it more expensive. (is)

C Choose a topic. Complete the sentences with information about yourself.

| drive to school   shop online |

Example: *Although driving to school is faster, I walk to school.*

I walk to school because it's healthier.

Although _____ , I _____ .

I _____ because _____ .

Lesson C Clauses of reason and concession

A Complete the sentences.

I bike to work	Jim keeps one in his backpack
I prefer to cook with one	Lucas uses one when he does laundry
I usually eat out	we wash our dishes by hand

1. Although an electric oven takes longer, *I prefer to cook with one* _____ .

2. Because an electronic dictionary is light, _____ .

3. Although a dryer is noisy, _____ .

4. Because dishwashers use a lot of water, _____ .

5. Because biking is good exercise, _____ .

6. Although I am an excellent cook, _____ .

B Correct the sentences. Add the missing word.

although	because	don't	have	he	is

1. Although *he* has a car, Sam takes the subway to work.

2. Frank talks to his friends over the Internet it is free.

3. Although they save a lot of time, I like electrical appliances.

4. Victor buys his lunch because he doesn't time to make one at home.

5. It is faster by subway, Joe and Mei-Lin drive to work.

6. We often buy food online although it more expensive.

C Choose two topics. Write sentences with information about yourself.
Use *because* and *although*.

drive to school	shop online	use a cell phone

Example: *Although driving to school is faster, I walk to school because it's healthier.*

1. _____

_____

2. _____

_____

Lesson C *Clauses of reason and concession*

A Match. Then combine the sentences. Use *because* or *although*.

1. An electric oven takes longer. __d__   a. We wash our dishes by hand.

2. An electronic dictionary is light. ____   b. I usually eat out.

3. A dryer is noisy. ____   c. I bike to work.

4. Dishwashers use a lot of water. ____   d. I prefer to cook with one.

5. Biking is good exercise. ____   e. Lucas uses one when he does laundry.

6. I am an excellent cook. ____   f. Jim keeps one in his backpack.

1. *Although an electric oven takes longer, I prefer to cook with one.*

2. _____

3. _____

4. _____

5. _____

6. _____

B Correct the sentences. Add the missing word.

1. Although ^he has a car, Sam takes the subway to work.

2. Frank talks to his friends over the Internet it is free.

3. Although they save a lot of time, I like electrical appliances.

4. Victor buys his lunch because he doesn't time to make one at home.

5. It is faster by subway, Joe and Mei-Lin drive to work.

6. We often buy food online although it more expensive.

C Choose three topics. Write sentences with information about yourself.
Use *because* and *although*.

drive to school   shop online   use a cell phone   (your own idea)

Example: *Although driving to school is faster, I walk to school because it's healthier.*

1. _____

   _____

2. _____

   _____

3. _____

   _____

A Skim the e-mail. Find the words in *italics*. Then circle the correct definition for each word.

1. amazing   (a.) fantastic   b. strange

2. outrageous   a. very high   b. unusual

3. virtual   a. online   b. almost real

4. reasonable   a. not expensive   b. intelligent

5. luckily   a. funnily   b. fortunately

6. popular   a. friendly   b. liked by a lot of people

B Read the e-mail. Match the questions with the answers.

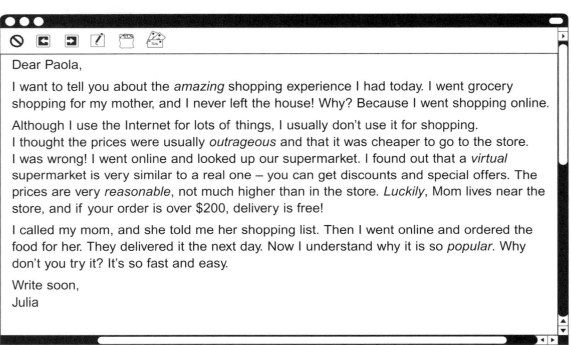

Dear Paola,

I want to tell you about the *amazing* shopping experience I had today. I went grocery shopping for my mother, and I never left the house! Why? Because I went shopping online.

Although I use the Internet for lots of things, I usually don't use it for shopping. I thought the prices were usually *outrageous* and that it was cheaper to go to the store. I was wrong! I went online and looked up our supermarket. I found out that a *virtual* supermarket is very similar to a real one – you can get discounts and special offers. The prices are very *reasonable*, not much higher than in the store. *Luckily*, Mom lives near the store, and if your order is over $200, delivery is free!

I called my mom, and she told me her shopping list. Then I went online and ordered the food for her. They delivered it the next day. Now I understand why it is so *popular*. Why don't you try it? It's so fast and easy.

Write soon,
Julia

1. What did Julia do for the first time? __c__   a. She thought it was amazing.

2. Why didn't she try it before? _____   b. You can save time and it's easy.

3. What did she find out about prices? _____   c. She bought groceries online.

4. What did she think of the experience? _____   d. They are very reasonable.

5. What are the benefits? _____   e. She thought it was too expensive.

A Skim the e-mail. Find the words in *italics*. Then match each word with the correct definition.

1. amazing __d__   a. very high

2. outrageous ____   b. fortunately

3. virtual ____   c. liked by a lot of people

4. reasonable ____   d. fantastic

5. luckily ____   e. online

6. popular ____   f. not expensive

B Read the e-mail. Answer the questions. Use the words in the box.

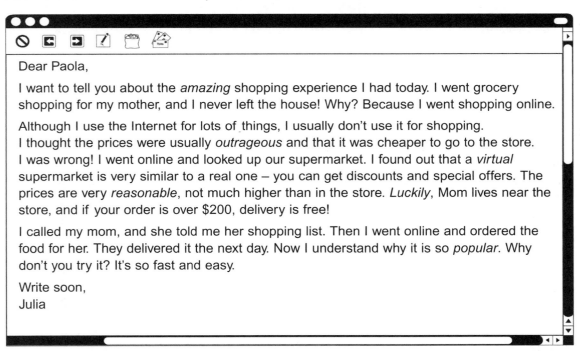

Dear Paola,

I want to tell you about the *amazing* shopping experience I had today. I went grocery shopping for my mother, and I never left the house! Why? Because I went shopping online.

Although I use the Internet for lots of things, I usually don't use it for shopping. I thought the prices were usually *outrageous* and that it was cheaper to go to the store. I was wrong! I went online and looked up our supermarket. I found out that a *virtual* supermarket is very similar to a real one – you can get discounts and special offers. The prices are very *reasonable*, not much higher than in the store. *Luckily*, Mom lives near the store, and if your order is over $200, delivery is free!

I called my mom, and she told me her shopping list. Then I went online and ordered the food for her. They delivered it the next day. Now I understand why it is so *popular*. Why don't you try it? It's so fast and easy.

Write soon,
Julia

amazing	expensive	fast	groceries	reasonable	time

1. What did Julia do for the first time? She bought _____*groceries*_____ online.

2. Why didn't she try it before? She thought it was too _____ .

3. What did she find out about prices? They are very _____ .

4. What did she think of the experience? She thought it was _____ .

5. What are the benefits? You can save _____ and it's _____ .

Lesson D Reading

■ ■ ☑

A Write a word for each definition.

1. fantastic   a _m_ _a_ z _i_ _n_ _g_

2. very high   o _ _ _ _ g _ _ _ s

3. online   v _ _ t _ _ _ _

4. not expensive   r _ _ s _ _ _ b _ _

5. fortunately   l _ _ k _ _ y

6. liked by a lot of people   p _ _ _ l _ _

B Complete the e-mail. Use the words from Exercise A. Then write questions.

> Dear Paola,
>
> I want to tell you about the _____ _amazing_ _____ shopping experience I had today. I went grocery shopping for my mother, and I never left the house! Why? Because I went shopping online.
>
> Although I use the Internet for lots of things, I usually don't use it for shopping. I thought the prices were usually _____ and that it was cheaper to go to the store. I was wrong! I went online and looked up our supermarket. I found out that a _____ supermarket is very similar to a real one – you can get discounts and special offers. The prices are very _____ , not much higher than in the store. _____ , Mom lives near the store, and if your order is over $200, delivery is free!
>
> I called my mom, and she told me her shopping list. Then I went online and ordered the food for her. They delivered it the next day. Now I understand why it is so _____ . Why don't you try it? It's so fast and easy.
>
> Write soon,
> Julia

1. (What / Julia / do / first time) _What did Julia do for the first time?_ _____

   Julia bought groceries online for the first time.

2. (Why / she / not try / before) _____

   She didn't try it before because she thought it was too expensive.

3. (What / she / find out / prices) _____

   She found out that they are very reasonable.

4. (What / she / think of / experience) _____

   She thought it was amazing.

5. (What / benefits) _____

   You can save time and it's easy.

Lesson E Writing

A Match each pair of positive and negative adjectives to the correct device.

+ easy to use	+ convenient	+ light
- noisy	- distracting	- expensive

1

cell phone

+ _convenient_

- _distracting_

2

dishwasher

+ _____

- _____

3

MP3 player

+ _____

- _____

B Read the diagram. Complete the sentences in the story.

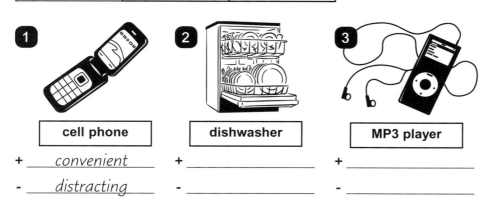

Online grocery shopping

can save time

Advantages

have to wait 1 or 2 days for delivery

Disadvantages

can stick to my budget

delivery for orders under $100 is expensive

My Favorite Time-saving Activity

My favorite time-saving activity is _online grocery shopping_ . Although I used to enjoy going to the store, it took a lot of time. I used to spend at least one evening a week on grocery shopping. Now I shop online. I _____ because I don't have to drive to the store, and I don't have to wait in line. Another benefit of online shopping is that I _____ (and my diet!) because I don't buy cookies or chips. One disadvantage is that I have to wait _____ . Another disadvantage is that _____ .

A Write one positive adjective and one negative adjective for each device.

| convenient | distracting | easy to use | expensive | light | noisy |

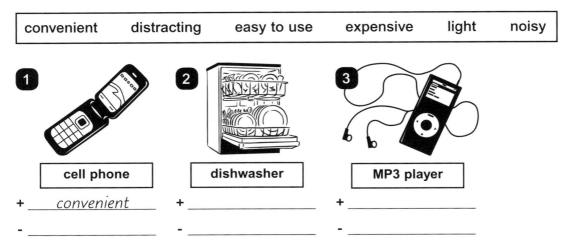

1 cell phone

2 dishwasher

3 MP3 player

+ _convenient_   + _____   + _____

- _____   - _____   - _____

B Complete the diagram. Use the information in the box. Then complete the sentences in the story.

| can save time | delivery for orders under $100 is expensive |
| can stick to my budget | have to wait 1 or 2 days for delivery |

can save time _____

Advantages

Online grocery shopping

Disadvantages

_____

_____   _____

My Favorite Time-saving Activity

My favorite time-saving activity is _online grocery shopping_ . Although I used to enjoy going to the store, it took a lot of time. I used to spend at least one evening a week on grocery shopping. Now I shop online. I _____ because I don't have to drive to the store, and I don't have to wait in line. Another benefit of online shopping is that I _____ (and my diet!) because I don't buy cookies or chips. One disadvantage is that I have to _____ _____ . Another disadvantage is that

_____ .

A Write one positive adjective and one negative adjective for each device. Add one more adjective and label it positive (+) or negative (-).

convenient	distracting	easy to use	expensive	light	noisy

1 cell phone

\+ *convenient*

\- _____

☐ _____

2 dishwasher

\+ _____

\- _____

☐ _____

3 MP3 player

\+ _____

\- _____

☐ _____

B Complete the diagram. Use your own ideas. Then complete the story.

Online grocery shopping

Advantages

Disadvantages

My Favorite Time-saving Activity

My favorite time-saving activity is *online grocery shopping* . Although I used to enjoy going to the store, it took a lot of time. I used to spend at least one evening a week on grocery shopping. Now I shop online. I _____ because _____ _____ . Another benefit of online shopping is that _____ because _____ . One disadvantage is that _____ . Another disadvantage is that _____ .

A Read the results of the survey. Circle the answers.

**Online Purchases by Students at Hall College
(Percentage of Students)**

Type of item	2005	2006	2007
1. Books	34	45	63
2. Clothes	29	31	40
3. Music	43	54	65
4. Groceries	12	15	10
5. Electrical appliances	7	15	9
6. Airline tickets	15	35	52

1. In 2005, the most popular product students bought online was _____ .
   (a.) music   b. books

2. In 2005, fewer than 10 percent of students used the Internet to buy _____ .
   a. groceries   b. electrical appliances

3. In 2007, buying books was less popular than buying _____ .
   a. clothes   b. music

4. From 2005 to 2007, there was a decline in the percentage of students
   who bought _____ online.
   a. groceries   b. airline tickets

5. From 2005 to 2007, the greatest increase was in buying _____ .
   a. books   b. airline tickets

6. In 2007, buying groceries was more popular than buying _____ .
   a. music   b. electrical appliances

B Choose an item from the survey. Complete the chart.

Item	Advantage of buying online	Disadvantage of buying online
Books	*You have a big choice of book titles.*	*You cannot skim parts of the book before you buy it.*

Lesson F Another view

A Read the results of the survey. Circle the answers.

**Online Purchases by Students at Hall College
(Percentage of Students)**

Type of item	2005	2006	2007
1. Books	34	45	63
2. Clothes	29	31	40
3. Music	43	54	65
4. Groceries	12	15	10
5. Electrical appliances	7	15	9
6. Airline tickets	15	35	52

1. In 2005, the most popular product students bought online was _____ .
   (a.) music   b. books   c. clothes

2. In 2005, fewer than 10 percent of students used the Internet to buy _____ .
   a. groceries   b. electrical appliances   c. airline tickets

3. In 2007, buying books was less popular than buying _____ .
   a. clothes   b. music   c. airline tickets

4. From 2005 to 2007, there was a decline in the percentage of students who bought _____ online.
   a. groceries   b. airline tickets   c. music

5. From 2005 to 2007, the greatest increase was in buying _____ .
   a. books   b. airline tickets   c. music

6. In 2007, buying groceries was more popular than buying _____ .
   a. music   b. electrical appliances   c. clothes

B Choose two items from the survey. Complete the chart.

Item	Advantage of buying online	Disadvantage of buying online
Books	You have a big choice of book titles.	You cannot skim parts of the book before you buy it.

Lesson **F** *Another view*

A Read the results of the survey. Complete the sentences.

**Online Purchases by Students at Hall College
(Percentage of Students)**

Type of item	2005	2006	2007
1. Books	34	45	63
2. Clothes	29	31	40
3. Music	43	54	65
4. Groceries	12	15	10
5. Electrical appliances	7	15	9
6. Airline tickets	15	35	52

1. In 2005, the most popular product students bought online was _____ *music* _____ .

2. In 2005, fewer than 10 percent of students used the Internet to buy

   _____ .

3. In 2007, buying books was less popular than buying _____ .

4. From 2005 to 2007, there was a decline in the percentage of students who bought

   _____ online.

5. From 2005 to 2007, the greatest increase was in buying _____ .

6. In 2007, buying groceries was more popular than buying _____ .

B Choose three items from the survey. Complete the chart.

Item	Advantage of buying online	Disadvantage of buying online
Books	*You have a big choice of book titles.*	*You cannot skim parts of the book before you buy it.*

Unit 7 Shopping

Lesson A Get ready

☑ ■ ■

A Circle the word that has the same meaning as the words in *italics*.

1. Could I *get my money back*?   (a.) get a refund   b. exchange
2. I'd like to *give back* this camera.   a. purchase   b. return
3. When did you *buy* it?   a. credit   b. purchase
4. What kind of *product* did you buy?   a. merchandise   b. policy
5. This device *does not work*.   a. is in bad condition   b. is defective
6. This is the store *rule*.   a. policy   b. warranty

B Complete the conversation.

customer service   defective   exchange   refund   store credit

Customer Excuse me. Is this ___customer service___ ?

Salesclerk Yes. How can I help you?

Customer I'd like to return this CD player. I'm not interested in an exchange.

Salesclerk Is it _____ ?

Customer No, it works fine. But it's just too complicated.

Salesclerk Are you sure you don't want to _____ it for a different CD player?

Customer No, thanks. Could I get a _____ , please?

Salesclerk I'm sorry. We don't give cash refunds. It's the store policy.

Customer I see. Well, please give me a _____ instead.

Salesclerk Could you please fill out this returned-merchandise form?

C Think of a situation when you returned something to a store. Complete the chart.

What did you buy?	
Why did you return it?	
What happened?	

Lesson A *Get ready*

■ ☑ ■

A Match the word that has the same meaning as the words in *italics*.

1. Could I *get my money back*? __c__   a. purchase
2. I'd like to *give back* this camera.   b. is defective
3. When did you *buy* it?   c. get a refund
4. What kind of *product* did you buy?   d. return
5. This device *does not work*.   e. policy
6. This is the store *rule*.   f. merchandise

B Complete the conversation.

customer service	exchange	refund	store credit
defective	policy	return	

Customer Excuse me. Is this ___customer service___ ?

Salesclerk Yes. How can I help you?

Customer I'd like to _____ this CD player. I'm not interested in an exchange.

Salesclerk Is it _____ ?

Customer No, it works fine. But it's just too complicated.

Salesclerk Are you sure you don't want to _____ it for a different CD player?

Customer No, thanks. Could I get a _____ , please?

Salesclerk I'm sorry. We don't give cash refunds. It's the store _____ .

Customer I see. Well, please give me a _____ instead.

Salesclerk Could you please fill out this returned-merchandise form?

C Think of a situation when you returned something to a store. Complete the chart.

What did you buy?	
Why did you return it?	
What happened?	
Did you like the store's return policy?	

Lesson A Get ready

A Write a word that has the same meaning as the words in *italics*.

1. Could I *get my money back*?   get a _r_ e _f_ _u_ _n_ _d_

2. I'd like to *give back* this camera.   _ _ _ _ _ n

3. When did you *buy* it?   _ _ r _ _ a _ _

4. What kind of *product* did you buy?   m _ _ c _ _ _ _ _ _ _ _

5. This device *does not work*.   is _ _ f _ c _ _ _ _

6. This is the store *rule*.   _ _ _ _ _ y

B Complete the conversation.

cash	defective	merchandise	refund	store credit
customer service	exchange	policy	return	

Customer Excuse me. Is this ___customer service___ ?

Salesclerk Yes. How can I help you?

Customer I'd like to _____ this CD player. I'm not interested in an exchange.

Salesclerk Is it _____ ?

Customer No, it works fine. But it's just too complicated.

Salesclerk Are you sure you don't want to _____ it for a different CD player?

Customer No, thanks. Could I get a _____ , please?

Salesclerk I'm sorry. We don't give _____ refunds. It's the store _____ .

Customer I see. Well, please give me a _____ instead.

Salesclerk Could you please fill out this returned-_____ form?

B Think of a situation when you returned something to a store. Complete the chart.

What did you buy?	
Why did you return it?	
What happened?	
Did you like the store's return policy?	

Lesson B Adjective clauses

Name: _____

☑ ■ ■

A Match.

1. I want to buy a camera that __c__ .
2. I'd like to buy some jeans that ____ .
3. I usually go to the supermarket that ____ .
4. The taxi driver who drove me home ____ .
5. Cell phones that ring loudly ____ .
6. The clerks who work at the computer store ____ .

a. aren't too expensive
b. is near my house
c. isn't very complicated
d. was very helpful
e. are very polite
f. are very annoying

B Correct the sentences. Add the missing word.

1. Terry wants to buy a laptop that ^is not too heavy. (is)
2. The store that near my house sells discount furniture. (is)
3. The salesclerk sold you this handbag is not here today. (who)
4. The cameras that in the window are on sale. (are)
5. Most people want to buy computers have a flat screen. (that)
6. I like supermarkets that a lot of good discounts. (have)

C What kind of people, clothes, and stores do you like? Complete the chart. Then complete the sentences.

People	Clothes	Stores
kind and friendly		

1. I like people who _are kind and friendly_____ .
2. I like clothes that _____ .
3. I like stores that _____ .

Name: _____

Lesson B Adjective clauses

■ ✓ ■

A Complete the sentences.

aren't too expensive	is near my house	ring loudly
drove me home	isn't very complicated	work at the computer store

1. I want to buy a camera that *isn't very complicated* _____ .

2. I'd like to buy some jeans that _____ .

3. I usually go to the supermarket that _____ .

4. The taxi driver who _____ was very helpful.

5. Cell phones that _____ are very annoying.

6. The clerks who _____ are very polite.

B Correct the sentences. Add the missing word.

are	have	is	is	that	who

1. Terry wants to buy a laptop that ^*is* not too heavy.

2. The store that near my house sells discount furniture.

3. The salesclerk sold you this handbag is not here today.

4. The cameras that in the window are on sale.

5. Most people want to buy computers have a flat screen.

6. I like supermarkets that a lot of good discounts.

C What kind of people, clothes, and stores do you like? Complete the chart. Then complete the sentences using adjective clauses.

People	Clothes	Stores
kind and friendly		

1. I like people *who are kind and friendly* _____ .

2. I like clothes _____ .

3. I like stores _____ .

Lesson B Adjective clauses

A Write new sentences. Use *that* or *who* and the words in the box to make adjective clauses.

aren't too expensive	is near my house	ring loudly
drove me home	isn't very complicated	work at the computer store

1. I want to buy a camera. *I want to buy a camera that isn't very complicated.*

2. I'd like to buy some jeans. _____

3. I usually go to the supermarket. _____

4. The taxi driver was very helpful. _____

5. Cell phones are very annoying. _____

6. The clerks are very polite. _____

B Correct the sentences. Add the missing word.

1. Terry wants to buy a laptop that ^*is* not too heavy.

2. The store that near my house sells discount furniture.

3. The salesclerk sold you this handbag is not here today.

4. The cameras that in the window are on sale.

5. Most people want to buy computers have a flat screen.

6. I like supermarkets that a lot of good discounts.

C What kind of people, clothes, and stores do you like? What kind do you dislike? Complete the chart. Then write sentences on a separate piece of paper. Use adjective clauses.

	People	Clothes	Stores
Like	*kind and friendly*		
Dislike	*not polite*		

Example: *I like people who are kind and friendly. I dislike people who are not polite.*

Lesson C Adjective clauses

A Complete the sentence about each item. Then label the pictures with the adjectives.

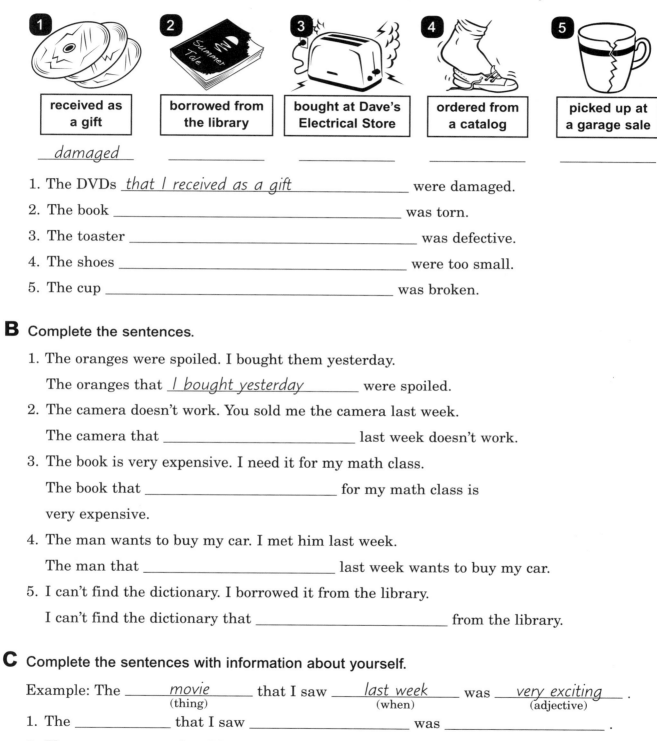

1	2	3	4	5
received as a gift	borrowed from the library	bought at Dave's Electrical Store	ordered from a catalog	picked up at a garage sale
damaged	_____	_____	_____	_____

1. The DVDs _that I received as a gift_____ were damaged.

2. The book _____ was torn.

3. The toaster _____ was defective.

4. The shoes _____ were too small.

5. The cup _____ was broken.

B Complete the sentences.

1. The oranges were spoiled. I bought them yesterday.

   The oranges that _I bought yesterday_____ were spoiled.

2. The camera doesn't work. You sold me the camera last week.

   The camera that _____ last week doesn't work.

3. The book is very expensive. I need it for my math class.

   The book that _____ for my math class is

   very expensive.

4. The man wants to buy my car. I met him last week.

   The man that _____ last week wants to buy my car.

5. I can't find the dictionary. I borrowed it from the library.

   I can't find the dictionary that _____ from the library.

C Complete the sentences with information about yourself.

Example: The _____movie_____ that I saw _____last week_____ was _____very exciting_____ .
           (thing)   (when)   (adjective)

1. The _____ that I saw _____ was _____ .

2. The _____ that I bought _____ was _____ .

Lesson C Adjective clauses

A Match the adjectives with the correct items. Then complete the sentences.

| broken | damaged | defective | too small | torn |

1 received as a gift **2** borrowed from the library **3** bought at Dave's Electrical Store **4** ordered from a catalog **5** picked up at a garage sale

damaged   _____   _____   _____   _____

1. The DVDs _that I received as a gift were damaged_ .
2. The book _____ .
3. The toaster _____ .
4. The shoes _____ .
5. The cup _____ .

B Combine the sentences. Change the second sentence into an adjective clause with *that*.

1. The oranges were spoiled. I bought them yesterday.

   The oranges that _I bought yesterday were spoiled._

2. The camera doesn't work. You sold me the camera last week.

   The camera that _____

3. The book is very expensive. I need it for my math class.

   The book that _____

4. The man wants to buy my car. I met him last week.

   The man that _____

5. I can't find the dictionary. I borrowed it from the library.

   I can't find _____

C Write sentences with information about yourself.

Example: _The movie that I saw last week was very exciting._

1. (saw) _____
2. (bought) _____

© Cambridge University Press 2009 **Photocopiable**

Lesson C Adjective clauses

Name: _____

A Match the adjectives with the correct items. Then complete the sentences.

broken	damaged	defective	too small	torn

1	2	3	4	5
received as a gift	borrowed from the library	bought at Dave's Electrical Store	ordered from a catalog	picked up at a garage sale
damaged	_____	_____	_____	_____

1. The DVDs _that I received as a gift were damaged_ .

2. The book _____ .

3. The toaster _____ .

4. The shoes _____ .

5. The cup _____ .

B Combine the sentences. Change the second sentence into an adjective clause with *that*.

1. The oranges were spoiled. I bought them yesterday.

   The oranges that I bought yesterday were spoiled.

2. The camera doesn't work. You sold me the camera last week.

   _____

3. The book is very expensive. I need it for my math class.

   _____

4. The man wants to buy my car. I met him last week.

   _____

5. I can't find the dictionary. I borrowed it from the library.

   _____

C Write sentences with information about yourself.

Example: _The movie that I saw last week was very exciting._

1. (saw) _____

2. (bought) _____

3. (ate) _____

A Match.

1. A person who loves books is a book __c__   a. policy.

2. A limit that is related to time is a time ____   b. refund.

3. A credit that is given by a store is a store ____   c. lover.

4. A refund that is made in cash is a cash ____   d. limit.

5. A policy that is about returns is a return ____   e. credit.

B Complete the newspaper advice column. Use the phrases from Exercise A.

Dear Smart Shopper,

    I am a _____ *book* _____ *lover* _____ , and I purchased some used books. Later, I found that two books had torn pages. I took them back, but the seller said that he didn't have to give me a _____ _____ because I bought them more than 28 days ago. He agreed to give me a _____ _____ . Why can't I get my money back?

Angry Arnold

Dear Angry Arnold,

    If the product is new and you find it is defective, you can ask for a refund. For used merchandise, it's the buyer's responsibility to check it carefully before buying. There may also be a _____ _____ for returns, so you should not wait. Always read the information on your receipt about the retailer's _____ _____ .

Smart Shopper

C Read the letters again. Circle the correct words.

1. Arnold was angry because his books were **damaged** / **defective**.

2. He did not know that there was a **cash refund** / **time limit** on returns.

3. The seller did not want to give Arnold a **store credit** / **cash refund**.

4. The seller gave Arnold a **return policy** / **store credit**.

5. He should read the receipt to learn about the **return policy** / **cash refund**.

Unit 7 Shopping

Lesson D *Reading*

Name: _____

A Complete the compound nouns.

1. A person who loves books is a book _____*lover*_____ .

2. A limit that is related to time is a time _____ .

3. A credit that is given by a store is a store _____ .

4. A refund that is made in cash is a cash _____ .

5. A policy that is about returns is a return _____ .

B Complete the newspaper advice column. Use the phrases from Exercise A and the words in the box.

defective	information	merchandise	responsibility	seller

Dear Smart Shopper,

I am a _*book*_ _*lover*_ , and I purchased some used books. Later, I found that two books had torn pages. I took them back, but the _____ said that he didn't have to give me a _____ _____ because I bought them more than 28 days ago. He agreed to give me a _____ _____ . Why can't I get my money back?

Angry Arnold

Dear Angry Arnold,

If the product is new and you find it is _____ , you can ask for a refund. For used _____ , it's the buyer's _____ to check it carefully before buying. There may also be a _____ _____ for returns, so you should not wait. Always read the _____ on your receipt about the retailer's _____ _____ .

Smart Shopper

C Read the letters again. Complete the sentences.

cash refund	damaged	return policy	store credit	time limit

1. Arnold was angry because his books were _*damaged*_ .

2. He did not know that there was a _____ on returns.

3. The seller did not want to give Arnold a _____ .

4. The seller gave Arnold a _____ .

5. He should read the receipt to learn about the _____ .

Lesson D *Reading*

Name: _____

A Complete the compound nouns.

1. A person who loves books is a ___book___ ___lover___ .

2. A limit that is related to time is a _____ _____ .

3. A credit that is given by a store is a _____ _____ .

4. A refund that is made in cash is a _____ _____ .

5. A policy that is about returns is a _____ _____ .

B Complete the newspaper advice column. Use the phrases from Exercise A and the words in the box.

Dear Smart Shopper,
I am a _book_ _lover_ , and I purchased some used books. Later, I found that two books had _____ pages. I took them back, but the _____ said that he didn't have to give me a _____ _____ because I bought them more than 28 days ago. He agreed to give me a _____ _____ . Why can't I get my _____ back?
Angry Arnold

| defective |
| merchandise |
| money |
| receipt |
| responsibility |
| seller |
| torn |

Dear Angry Arnold,
If the product is new and you find it is _____ , you can ask for a refund. For used _____ , it's the buyer's _____ to check it carefully before buying. There may also be a _____ _____ for returns, so you should not wait. Always read the information on your _____ about the retailer's _____ _____ .
Smart Shopper

C Read the letters again. Complete the sentences.

1. Arnold was angry because his books were ___damaged___ .

2. He did not know that there was a _____ on returns.

3. The seller did not want to give Arnold a _____ .

4. The seller gave Arnold a _____ .

5. He should read the receipt to learn about the _____ .

A Complete the chart.

You can pay later.	You get a large bill once a month.
You can spend too much.	You get a record of your purchases.
You don't need cash.	You pay a lot of interest.

Why you should use a credit card	**Why you shouldn't use a credit card**
You can pay later.	*You can spend too much.*

B Circle the correct words.

Why You Should Use a Credit Card

There are some good reasons why you should use a credit card when you go shopping. **Second** /**First**, you can pay later instead of when you purchase the item. **Second** / **Finally**, you don't need to have cash with you, so it is safer. **Second** / **Next**, you get a record of your purchases. **Second** / **Finally**, you have a guarantee of a refund or replacement if the merchandise is defective.

C Complete the paragraph. Use the sentences from Exercise A. Use Exercise B as a model.

Why You Shouldn't Use a Credit Card

There are some good reasons why you shouldn't use a credit card when you go shopping. First, _____ .

Second, _____

_____ . Finally, _____

_____ .

Lesson E Writing

Name: _____

A Complete the chart. Add two more sentences.

You can pay later.	You get a large bill once a month.
You can spend too much.	You get a record of your purchases.
You don't need cash.	You pay a lot of interest.

Why you should use a credit card	Why you shouldn't use a credit card
You can pay later.	

B Complete the sentences.

Finally	First	Next	Second

Why You Should Use a Credit Card

There are some good reasons why you should use a credit card when you go shopping. _____First_____ , you can pay later instead of when you purchase the item. _____2_____ , you don't need to have cash with you, so it is safer. _____3_____ , you get a record of your purchases. _____4_____ , you have a guarantee of a refund or replacement if the merchandise is defective.

C Write a paragraph on the topic below. Use the back of this paper. Use the sentences from Exercise A and *First*, *Second*, and *Finally*. Start like this.

Why You Shouldn't Use a Credit Card

There are some good reasons why you shouldn't use a credit card when you go shopping.

Name: _____

A Complete the chart. Add four more sentences.

You can pay later.	You get a large bill once a month.
You can spend too much.	You get a record of your purchases.
You don't need cash.	You pay a lot of interest.

Why you should use a credit card	Why you shouldn't use a credit card
You can pay later.	

B Complete the sentences. Use transition words.

Why You Should Use a Credit Card

There are some good reasons why you should use a credit card when you go shopping. _____*First*_____ , you can pay later instead of when you
1
purchase the item. _____ , you don't need to have cash with
2
you, so it is safer. _____ , you get a record of your purchases.
3
_____ , if you buy something with a credit card, you have a
4
guarantee of a refund or replacement if the merchandise is defective.

C Write a paragraph on the topic below. Use the back of this paper. Use the sentences from Exercise A and transition words, and add your own ideas. Start like this.

Why You Shouldn't Use a Credit Card

There are some good reasons why you shouldn't use a credit card when you go shopping.

A Read the return policy. Circle the answers.

EAST SIDE OFFICE EMPORIUM RETURN POLICY

If you paid with cash, debit card, or check and you have your receipt, we will refund your purchase with cash if it was an in-store purchase or by check if it was an online purchase.

If your purchase cost more than $500 and you paid with cash, debit card, or check, we will refund your money with a check if you have your receipt. If you paid by credit card and have your receipt, we will credit your account.

If you do not have your receipt, we will give you a store credit for the current selling price.

You must return your purchase in new condition with the original packaging, including manuals and parts. There is a 28-day time limit on all returns.

1. Two weeks ago, Katerina bought an office chair in the store for $85. Now she wants to return it. She has her receipt and she paid by check. What type of refund will she get?

    (a.) a cash refund   b. a refund by check

2. Three weeks ago, Tuan bought a laptop in the store for $695. Now he wants to return it. He doesn't have his receipt. He paid by credit card. What type of refund will he get?

    a. no refund   b. a store credit

3. Six weeks ago, Ramon bought a lamp on the Internet for $45. Now he wants to return it. He has his receipt. He paid by credit card. What type of refund will he get?

    a. a credit to his account   b. no refund

4. Last week, Francesca bought a printer on the Internet for $99. Now she wants to return it. She has her receipt and she paid by debit card. What type of refund will she get?

    a. a cash refund   b. a refund by check

B Match the parts of the conversations.

1. Was your jacket expensive? __c__   a. No, it was marked down.

2. Did you pay the full price for this CD? ____   b. No, it's a real lemon.

3. Did it take long to find this lamp? ____   c. Yes, it cost a fortune.

4. Do you like the used car you bought? ____   d. Yes, I had to shop around for it.

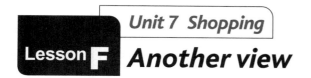

Name: _____

A Read the return policy. Circle the answers.

EAST SIDE OFFICE EMPORIUM RETURN POLICY

If you paid with cash, debit card, or check and you have your receipt, we will refund your purchase with cash if it was an in-store purchase or by check if it was an online purchase.

If your purchase cost more than $500 and you paid with cash, debit card, or check, we will refund your money with a check if you have your receipt. If you paid by credit card and have your receipt, we will credit your account.

If you do not have your receipt, we will give you a store credit for the current selling price.

You must return your purchase in new condition with the original packaging, including manuals and parts. There is a 28-day time limit on all returns.

---

1. Two weeks ago, Katerina bought an office chair in the store for $85. Now she wants to return it. She has her receipt and she paid by check. What type of refund will she get?

   (a.) a cash refund   b. a refund by check   c. a store credit

2. Three weeks ago, Tuan bought a laptop in the store for $695. Now he wants to return it. He doesn't have his receipt. He paid by credit card. What type of refund will he get?

   a. no refund   b. a store credit   c. a cash refund

3. Six weeks ago, Ramon bought a lamp on the Internet for $45. Now he wants to return it. He has his receipt. He paid by credit card. What type of refund will he get?

   a. a credit to his account   b. no refund   c. a cash refund

4. Last week, Francesca bought a printer on the Internet for $99. Now she wants to return it. She has her receipt and she paid by debit card. What type of refund will she get?

   a. a cash refund   b. a refund by check   c. a store credit

B Complete the conversations.

fortune	lemon	marked down	shop around

1. Was your jacket expensive?   Yes, it cost a _____*fortune*_____ .

2. Did you pay the full price for this CD?   No, it was _____ .

3. Did it take long to find this lamp?   Yes, I had to _____ for it.

4. Do you like the used car you bought?   No, it's a real _____ .

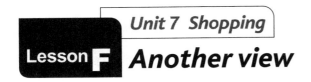

Unit 7 Shopping

Lesson F Another view

A Read the information and answer the questions.

EAST SIDE OFFICE EMPORIUM RETURN POLICY

If you paid with cash, debit card, or check and you have your receipt, we will refund your purchase with cash if it was an in-store purchase or by check if it was an online purchase.

If your purchase cost more than $500 and you paid with cash, debit card, or check, we will refund your money with a check if you have your receipt. If you paid by credit card and have your receipt, we will credit your account.

If you do not have your receipt, we will give you a store credit for the current selling price.

You must return your purchase in new condition with the original packaging, including manuals and parts. There is a 28-day time limit on all returns.

---

1. Two weeks ago, Katerina bought an office chair in the store for $85. Now she wants to return it. She has her receipt and she paid by check. What type of refund will she get?

   She will get a cash refund.

2. Three weeks ago, Tuan bought a laptop in the store for $695. Now he wants to return it. He doesn't have his receipt. He paid by credit card. What type of refund will he get?

   _____

3. Six weeks ago, Ramon bought a lamp on the Internet for $45. Now he wants to return it. He has his receipt. He paid by credit card. What type of refund will he get?

   _____

4. Last week, Francesca bought a printer on the Internet for $99. Now she wants to return it. She has her receipt and she paid by debit card. What type of refund will she get?

   _____

B Think of another way to say each hint. Then complete the conversations.

Hints:	1. a lot of money	2. reduced	3. look in many stores	4. a fruit

1. Was your jacket expensive?   Yes, it cost a *fortune* .

2. Did you pay the full price for this CD?   No, it was _____ _____ .

3. Did it take long to find this lamp?   Yes, I had to _____ _____ for it.

4. Do you like the used car you bought?   No, it's a real _____ .

© Cambridge University Press 2009 **Photocopiable**

A Circle the word or phrase that has the same meaning as the words in *italics*.

1. We need to *find a solution*.   (a.) work it out   b. share

2. Write *the first letters of your name* here.   a. your initials   b. tasks

3. Trisha is *very tired*.   a. frustrated   b. exhausted

4. He doesn't want to *reach an agreement*.   a. give advice   b. negotiate

5. We have to *take responsibility for* the problem.   a. deal with   b. work it out

6. She doesn't want to do her *part* of the project.   a. share   b. agree

B Complete the conversations. Use the answers from Exercise A.

1. **A** Did you reach an agreement with your customer?

   B No, I didn't. I'll have to __negotiate__ with him again tomorrow.

2. **A** Are you going to tell your boss about the problem?

   B No, I'm going to try to _____ it _____ with my co-worker first.

3. **A** I always do more work than you!

   B No, you don't. I always do my _____ .

4. **A** My co-worker always leaves work early. What should I do?

   B You should ask your boss to _____ _____ it.

5. **A** What is the chart for?

   B We have to write our job duties and our _____ on it.

6. **A** How are you feeling today?

   B I'm completely _____ .

C Read the problems. Circle the best solution.

1. Sam has to work late every night because he has too much work. His wife and family are not happy. What should he do?

   a. Talk to his boss.   b. Talk to his co-workers.

2. Ling's co-workers don't talk to him. They don't invite him for coffee or lunch. What should he do?

   a. Talk to his boss.   b. Talk to his co-workers.

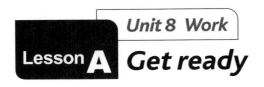

A Write the word or phrase that has the same meaning as the words in *italics*.

deal with	exhausted	negotiate	share	work it out	your initials

1. We need to *find a solution*.   *work it out*

2. Write *the first letters of your name* here.   _____

3. Trisha is *very tired*.   _____

4. He doesn't want to *reach an agreement*.   _____

5. We have to *take responsibility for* the problem.   _____

6. She doesn't want to do her *part* of the project.   _____

B Match a sentence in Part A with a sentence in Part B to make conversations.

Part A

1. Did you reach an agreement with your customer? _*a*_

2. Are you going to tell your boss about the problem? _____

3. I always do more work than you! _____

4. My co-worker always leaves work early. What should I do? _____

5. What is the chart for? _____

6. How are you feeling today? _____

Part B

a. No, I didn't. I'll have to negotiate with him again tomorrow.

b. We have to write our job duties and our initials on it.

c. You should ask your boss to deal with it.

d. No, you don't. I always do my share.

e. I'm completely exhausted.

f. No, I'm going to try to work it out with my co-worker first.

C Read the problems. Circle the best solution, or write your own.

1. Sam has to work late every night because he has too much work. His wife
   and family are not happy. What should he do?
   a. Talk to his boss.   b. Talk to his co-workers.   c. Other _____

2. Ling's co-workers don't talk to him. They don't invite him for coffee or lunch.
   What should he do?
   a. Talk to his boss.   b. Talk to his co-workers.   c. Other _____

Name: _____

A Complete words with the same meaning as the words in *italics*.

1. We need to *find a solution*.   w _o_ _r_ _k_ it out

2. Write *the first letters of your name* here.   your i__ __ __ __ __ __ __

3. Trisha is *very tired*.   ex__ __ __ __ __ __ __

4. He doesn't want to *reach an agreement*.   n__g__ __ __ __ __ __

5. We have to *take responsibility for* the problem. d__ __ __ with

6. She doesn't want to do her *part* of the project. s__ __ __ __

B Complete the sentences in Part B. Use the words from Exercise A. Then match a sentence in Part A with a sentence in Part B to make conversations.

Part A

1. Did you reach an agreement with your customer? _a_

2. Are you going to tell your boss about the problem? ____

3. I always do more work than you! ____

4. My co-worker always leaves work early. What should I do? ____

5. What is the chart for? ____

6. How are you feeling today? ____

Part B

a. No, I didn't. I'll have to __negotiate__ with him again tomorrow.

b. We have to write our job duties and our _____ on it.

c. You should ask your boss to _____ _____ it.

d. No, you don't. I always do my _____ .

e. I'm completely _____ .

f. No, I'm going to try to _____ it _____ with my co-worker first.

C Read the problems. Write solutions

1. Sam has to work late every night because he has too much work. His wife and family are not happy. What should he do?

_____

2. Ling's co-workers don't talk to him. They don't invite him for coffee or lunch. What should he do?

_____

Name: _____

Lesson B *Tense contrast*

A Match the sentences about the Gomez family.

4:00 p.m.–5:30 p.m.

Luisa / do her
homework

5:00 p.m.–6:00 p.m.

Mary / talk on the
phone

5:30 p.m.–6:30 p.m.

Pete / cook dinner

6:30 p.m.–7:30 p.m.

Pete, Luisa, and
Mary / eat dinner

1. It's 4:30 p.m. Luisa __c__

2. It's 5:15 p.m. Mary _____

3. It's 5:30 p.m. Luisa _____

4. It's 6:00 p.m. Mary _____

5. It's 6:10 p.m. Pete _____

6. It's 6:30 p.m. Pete _____

7. It's 6:40 p.m. Pete, Luisa, and Mary _____

8. It's 7:35 p.m. Pete, Luisa, and Mary _____

a. has been cooking dinner for 40 minutes.

b. have been eating dinner for 10 minutes.

c. has been doing her homework for 30 minutes.

d. have eaten dinner.

e. has finished talking on the phone.

f. has been talking on the phone for 15 minutes.

g. has done her homework.

h. has finished cooking dinner.

B Circle the correct words.

1. Pam has been **baking** / **baked** bread for two hours.

2. Gino and Teresa have been **cleaning** / **cleaned** the windows for one hour.

3. We have just **opening** / **opened** the front door of the store.

4. Tam and Luis have **finishing** / **finished** eating breakfast.

5. I have been **talking** / **talked** on the phone for 20 minutes.

6. Sonya has just **arriving** / **arrived** at work.

C Complete the chart.

It is Saturday at 11:00 a.m. What are you doing now?	It is Saturday at 11:00 p.m. What are you doing now?

Lesson B *Tense contrast*

A Complete the sentences about the Gomez family.

| 4:00 p.m.–5:30 p.m. | 5:00 p.m.–6:00 p.m. | 5:30 p.m.–6:30 p.m. | 6:30 p.m.–7:30 p.m. |

Luisa / do her homework   Mary / talk on the phone   Pete / cook dinner   Pete, Luisa, and Mary / eat dinner

1. It's 4:30 p.m. Luisa _____*has been*_____ doing her homework for 30 minutes.

2. It's 5:15 p.m. Mary _____ talking on the phone for 15 minutes.

3. It's 5:30 p.m. Luisa _____ done her homework.

4. It's 6:00 p.m. Mary _____ finished talking on the phone.

5. It's 6:10 p.m. Pete _____ cooking dinner for 40 minutes.

6. It's 6:30 p.m. Pete _____ finished cooking dinner.

7. It's 6:40 p.m. Pete, Luisa, and Mary _____ eating dinner for 10 minutes.

8. It's 7:35 p.m. Pete, Luisa, and Mary _____ eaten dinner.

B Circle the correct words.

1. Pam **(has been baking)** / **has baked** bread for two hours.

2. Gino and Teresa **have been cleaning** / **have cleaned** the windows for one hour.

3. We **have been opening** / **have just opened** the front door of the store.

4. Tam and Luis **have been finishing** / **have finished** eating breakfast.

5. I **have been talking** / **have talked** on the phone for 20 minutes.

6. Sonya **has been arriving** / **has just arrived** at work.

C Complete the chart.

	It is Saturday at 11:00 a.m. What are you doing now?	It is Saturday at 11:00 p.m. What are you doing now?	
You			
Your friend			

A Complete the sentences about the Gomez family. Use the present perfect or present perfect continuous.

| 4:00 p.m.–5:30 p.m. | 5:00 p.m.–6:00 p.m. | 5:30 p.m.–6:30 p.m. | 6:30 p.m.–7:30 p.m. |

Luisa / do her homework   Mary / talk on the phone   Pete / cook dinner   Pete, Luisa, and Mary / eat dinner

1. It's 4:30 p.m. Luisa _____*has been doing*_____ her homework for 30 minutes.

2. It's 5:15 p.m. Mary _____ on the phone for 15 minutes.

3. It's 5:30 p.m. Luisa _____ her homework.

4. It's 6:00 p.m. Mary _____ talking on the phone.

5. It's 6:10 p.m. Pete _____ dinner for 40 minutes.

6. It's 6:30 p.m. Pete _____ dinner.

7. It's 6:40 p.m. Pete, Luisa, and Mary _____ dinner for 10 minutes.

8. It's 7:35 p.m. Pete, Luisa, and Mary _____ dinner.

B Complete the sentences.

1. Pam _____*has been baking*_____ bread for two hours.
   (bake)

2. Gino and Teresa _____ the windows for one hour.
   (clean)

3. We _____ the front door of the store.
   (open)

4. Tam and Luis _____ eating breakfast.
   (finish)

5. I _____ on the phone for 20 minutes.
   (talk)

6. Sonya _____ at work.
   (arrive)

C Complete the chart.

	It is Saturday at 11:00 a.m. What are you doing now?	It is Saturday at 11:00 p.m. What are you doing now?
You		
Your friend		

Lesson C *Participipial adjectives*

A Circle the correct adjective.

1. We were _____ to go to Jan's birthday party.
   (a.) excited   b. frustrated

2. I was _____ because the job did not pay well.
   a. disappointed   b. interested

3. The stories were not funny, and we were _____ .
   a. amused   b. bored

4. The work was too difficult, and we felt _____ .
   a. fascinated   b. frustrated

5. The storm was dangerous, and I was _____ .
   a. frightened   b. disappointed

6. The computers could do amazing things, and we were _____ .
   a. bored   b. fascinated

B Write the correct adjective.

A Working Weekend

Last weekend, my co-workers and I had special training. I thought it was

going to be ___*interesting*___ but very _____ . On
     1. interested / interesting   2. tired / tiring

Saturday afternoon, I felt like going to sleep in the meetings because they were

so _____ . The teacher was _____ because
    3. bored / boring   4. irritated / irritating

we didn't ask many questions. At the end of the day, there was a party. The party

was much more _____ than the meetings, but I didn't eat
       5. excited / exciting

much because the food was _____ . We danced and talked
          6. disappointed / disappointing

a lot at the party, and at the end of the night we were _____ .
                      7. exhausted / exhausting

Everyone was _____ when we came back to work on Monday
    8. amused / amusing

and told our stories.

C Think about activities that you do in your job or at home. Write a sentence.

Example: (interesting) *Talking to customers is interesting because I meet different people.*

(interesting) _____

Lesson **C** *Participial adjectives*

■☑■

A Complete the sentences.

| bored | disappointed | excited | fascinated | frightened | frustrated |

1. We were _____*excited*_____ to go to Jan's birthday party.

2. I was _____ because the job did not pay well.

3. The stories were not funny, and we were _____ .

4. The work was too difficult, and we felt _____ .

5. The storm was dangerous, and I was _____ .

6. The computers could do amazing things, and we were _____ .

B Complete the story. Use the words in the box.

| amused | disappointing | exhausted | irritated |
| boring | exciting | interesting | tiring |

A Working Weekend

Last weekend, my co-workers and I had special training. I thought it was

going to be _____*interesting*_____ but very _____ . On
                          1   2

Saturday afternoon, I felt like going to sleep in the meetings because they were

so _____ . The teacher was _____ because
              3   4

we didn't ask many questions. At the end of the day, there was a party. The party

was much more _____ than the meetings, but I didn't eat
                          5

much because the food was _____ . We danced and talked
                                        6

a lot at the party, and at the end of the night we were _____ .
                                                                      7

Everyone was _____ when we came back to work on Monday
                          8

and told our stories.

C Think about activities that you do in your job or at home. Write two sentences.

Example: (interesting) *Talking to customers is interesting because I meet different people.*

1. (interesting) _____

2. (boring) _____

Lesson C Participial adjectives

A Complete the sentences.

1. We were e<u> x </u><u> c </u><u> i </u><u> t </u><u> e </u><u> d </u> to go to Jan's birthday party.

2. I was dis__ __ __ __ __ __ __ __ __ because the job did not pay well.

3. The stories were not funny, and we were bo__ __ __ .

4. The work was too difficult, and we felt fr__ __ __ __ __ __ __ __ .

5. The storm was dangerous, and I was fr__ __ __ __ __ __ __ __ .

6. The computers could do amazing things, and we were fas__ __ __ __ __ __ __ .

B Complete the story. Use the correct adjective form of the words in the box.

amuse	disappoint	exhaust	irritate
bore	excite	interest	tire

A Working Weekend

Last weekend, my co-workers and I had special training. I thought it was

going to be _____*interesting*_____ but very _____ . On
                    1   2

Saturday afternoon, I felt like going to sleep in the meetings because they were

so _____ . The teacher was _____ because
              3   4

we didn't ask many questions. At the end of the day, there was a party. The party

was much more _____ than the meetings, but I didn't eat
                        5

much because the food was _____ . We danced and talked
                                      6

a lot at the party, and at the end of the night we were _____ .
                                                                  7

Everyone was _____ when we came back to work on Monday
                      8

and told our stories.

C Think about activities that you do in your job or at home. Write three sentences.

Example: (interesting) <u>*Talking to customers is interesting because I meet different people.*</u>

1. (interesting) _____

2. (boring) _____

3. (exciting) _____

A Write the skills in the chart.

Arrives on time	Can fix equipment	Can use a computer	Is honest

Hard job skills	Soft job skills
Can fix equipment	

B Read. Then choose the soft skill that matches each of the numbered sentences.

Soft Skills on the Job

Eugenia has been working at the Island Sports Club for two months. She works at the front desk. (1) She is always friendly and polite to the customers. At first, she didn't always understand the manager's instructions, but she asked lots of questions. (2) She is always on time for work and always finishes her tasks. (3) When her boss criticizes her, she doesn't complain. "She enjoys learning about the job," explains Margery Vincent, manager of Island Sports Club. (4) "She's always cheerful and optimistic. The customers like her." (5) Eugenia gets along well with her co-workers, too. Now they ask her for help and advice.

1. a. has good communication skills   b. has a strong work ethic

2. a. is a team player   b. has a strong work ethic

3. a. is honest   b. learns from criticism

4. a. has good communication skills   b. has a positive attitude

5. a. is a team player   b. is honest

C Think about the soft skills you need at your job or at a job you want to have. Write the information.

Job: _____

1. You need to be _____ .

2. You need to have _____ .

Name: _____

A Write the skills in the chart.

Arrives on time	Can use a computer	Is honest
Can fix equipment	Is friendly	Speaks other languages

Hard job skills	Soft job skills
Can fix equipment	

B Read. Write the number of the sentence that is an example of each soft skill.

Soft Skills on the Job

Eugenia has been working at the Island Sports Club for two months. She works at the front desk. (1) She is always friendly and polite to the customers. At first, she didn't always understand the manager's instructions, but she asked lots of questions. (2) She is always on time for work and always finishes her tasks. (3) When her boss criticizes her, she doesn't complain. "She enjoys learning about the job," explains Margery Vincent, manager of Island Sports Club. (4) "She's always cheerful and optimistic. The customers like her." (5) Eugenia gets along well with her co-workers, too. Now they ask her for help and advice.

Has good communication skills __1__   Learns from criticism _____

Has a positive attitude _____   Is a team player _____

Has a strong work ethic _____

C Think about the soft skills you need at your job or at a job you want to have. Write the information.

Job: _____

1. You need to be _____ .

2. You need to have _____ .

3. It's important to _____ .

A Write the skills in the chart.

Arrives on time	Is friendly	Is honest
Can fix equipment	Is good at math	Speaks other languages
Can use a computer	Is good at talking to people	

Hard job skills	Soft job skills
Can fix equipment	

B Read. Write an example from the text for each soft skill.

Soft Skills on the Job

Eugenia has been working at the Island Sports Club for two months. She works at the front desk. She is always friendly and polite to the customers. At first, she didn't always understand the manager's instructions, but she asked lots of questions. She is always on time for work and always finishes her tasks. When her boss criticizes her, she doesn't complain. "She enjoys learning about the job," explains Margery Vincent, manager of Island Sports Club. "She's always cheerful and optimistic. The customers like her." Eugenia gets along well with her co-workers, too. Now they ask her for help and advice.

1. Has good communication skills *She is always friendly and polite to the customers.*

2. Has a strong work ethic _____

3. Learns from criticism _____

4. Has a positive attitude _____

5. Is a team player _____

C Think about the soft skills you need at your job or at a job you want to have. Write the information on the back of this paper.

A Complete the letter.

enclosed	get along	interested	position	skilled

Eugenia Chang
458 North Main St.
Providence, RI 02906
August 8, 2008

Edmilson Ferreira, Sports Coordinator
Capital Athletics
356 Farmington Ave.
Hartford, CT 06108

Dear Mr. Ferreira:

I read your advertisement online for a _____*position*_____ as a sports

instructor. I am very _____ in this position, and I have

_____ my resume.

I have been working as a front desk manager at Island Sports for 18 months.

In this job, I have learned how to help customers use the sports equipment. I am

_____ at teaching many sports. I also _____

well with my co-workers.

I am looking for an opportunity to learn more and take on more responsibility in my

job. I look forward to hearing from you.

Sincerely,

Eugenia Chang

Eugenia Chang

B Read about a job and an applicant interested in the job. Write a cover letter on a separate piece of paper with the information. Use Exercise A as a model.

Job ad	Information about applicant
Front desk manager needed. Sports training or experience preferred. Apply to: Margery Vincent, Manager Island Sports Club P.O. Box 4567, Providence, RI 02903	Name: Julio Alvarez Address: 5 Elk Dr., Cranston, RI 02921 Current job: Coach at Cole High School Skills: Can coach volleyball and baseball. Enjoys helping people.

A Complete the letter.

| been working | get along | look forward | skilled |
| enclosed | have learned | position | very interested |

Eugenia Chang
458 North Main St.
Providence, RI 02906
August 8, 2008

Edmilson Ferreira, Sports Coordinator
Capital Athletics
356 Farmington Ave.
Hartford, CT 06108

Dear Mr. Ferreira:

I read your advertisement online for a _____*position*_____ as a

sports instructor. I am _____ in this position, and I have

_____ my resume.

I have _____ as a front desk manager at Island Sports for

18 months. In this job, I _____ how to help customers use the

sports equipment. I am _____ at teaching many sports. I also

_____ well with my co-workers.

I am looking for an opportunity to learn more and take on more responsibility in my

job. I _____ to hearing from you.

Sincerely,

Eugenia Chang
Eugenia Chang

B Read about a job and an applicant interested in the job. Write a cover letter on a separate piece of paper with the information. Use Exercise A as a model.

Job ad	Information about applicant
Front desk manager needed. Sports training or experience preferred. Apply to: Margery Vincent, Manager Island Sports Club P.O. Box 4567, Providence, RI 02903	Name: Julio Alvarez Address: 5 Elk Dr., Cranston, RI 02921 Current job: Coach at Cole High School Skills: Can coach volleyball and baseball. Enjoys helping people and has a positive attitude.

A Complete the sentences. Then write the sentences in the correct places in the letter.

hearing from you	my co-workers	teaching many sports
in this position	my resume	

1. I am very interested *in this position* .

4. I also get along well with _____ .

2. I have enclosed _____ .

5. I look forward to _____ .

3. I am skilled at _____ .

Eugenia Chang
458 North Main St.
Providence, RI 02906
August 8, 2008

Edmilson Ferreira, Sports Coordinator
Capital Athletics
356 Farmington Ave.
Hartford, CT 06108

Dear Mr. Ferreira:

I read your advertisement online for a position as a sports instructor. *I am very interested in this position* , and _____

_____ .

I have been working as a front desk manager at Island Sports for 18 months. In this job, I have learned how to help customers use the sports equipment. _____

_____ . _____ .

I am looking for an opportunity to learn more and take on more responsibility in my job. _____ .

Sincerely,

Eugenia Chang

Eugenia Chang

B Read about a job. Make up information about an applicant. Then write a cover letter on a separate piece of paper with the information. Use Exercise A as a model.

Job ad	Information about applicant
Front desk manager needed. Sports training or experience preferred. Apply to: Margery Vincent, Manager Island Sports Club P.O. Box 4567, Providence, RI 02903	Name: Julio Alvarez Address: 5 Elk Dr., Cranston, RI 02921 Current job: _____ Skills: _____ _____

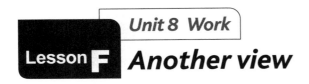

Lesson F Another view

A Match the sentences with the soft skills.

1. I usually speak a lot when I work with others in a group. _d_

2. I usually make a schedule for the week. ____

3. I am good at writing reports. ____

4. I usually ask questions about my job duties. ____

5. I prefer to have written instructions. ____

a. understand instructions
b. manage time
c. reading comprehension
d. verbal communication
e. written communication

B Read the job descriptions. Circle the soft skill that is *not* required for each job.

1. **Doctor**: listen to patients, explain medications, schedule appointments

   verbal communication / (written communication)

2. **Sales assistant**: answer e-mails, follow manager's instructions, fill out forms

   written communication / manage time

3. **Hotel manager**: help customers, answer the phone, train assistant managers

   teach others / reading comprehension

4. **Waiter**: help customers, take phone orders, plan weekly schedules for staff

   manage time / teach others

C Choose one soft skill from Exercise A. Give one example of why you are good at this skill.

Skill: _____

Example: _____

_____

A Match the sentences with the soft skills.

1. I usually speak a lot when I work with others in a group. _d_
2. I usually make a schedule for the week. ____
3. I am good at writing reports. ____
4. I usually ask questions about my job duties. ____
5. I prefer to have written instructions. ____
6. I always act professionally and do my work carefully. ____
7. I enjoy giving instructions to new employees. ____

a. understand instructions
b. manage time
c. reading comprehension
d. verbal communication
e. written communication
f. teach others
g. strong work ethic

B Read the job descriptions. Circle the soft skill that is *not* required for each job.

1. **Doctor**: listen to patients, explain medications, schedule appointments
   a. verbal communication   b. manage time   (c.) written communication

2. **Sales assistant**: answer e-mails, follow manager's instructions, fill out forms
   a. written communication   b. understand instructions   c. manage time

3. **Hotel manager**: help customers, answer the phone, train assistant managers
   a. teach others   b. reading comprehension   c. verbal communication

4. **Waiter**: help customers, take phone orders, plan weekly schedules for staff
   a. manage time   b. verbal communication   c. teach others

C Choose one soft skill from Exercise A. Give two examples of why you are good at this skill.

Skill: _____

Examples:

1. _____

2. _____

Name: _____

A Match the sentences with the soft skills. Use some skills twice.

1. I usually speak a lot when I work with others in a group. _d_

2. I usually make a schedule for the week. ____

3. I am good at writing reports. ____

4. I usually ask questions about my job duties. ____

5. I prefer to have written instructions. ____

6. I always act professionally and do my work carefully. ____

7. I enjoy giving instructions to new employees. ____

8. I am good at talking to customers on the phone. ____

9. I am always on time for meetings. ____

a. understand instructions

b. manage time

c. reading comprehension

d. verbal communication

e. written communication

f. teach others

g. strong work ethic

B Read the job descriptions. Look at the soft skills in Exercise A. Write a soft skill that is *not* required for each job.

1. **Doctor**: listen to patients, explain medications, schedule appointments
   written communication

2. **Sales assistant**: answer e-mails, follow manager's instructions, fill out forms
   _____

3. **Hotel manager**: help customers, answer the phone, train assistant managers
   _____

4. **Waiter**: help customers, take phone orders, plan weekly schedules for staff
   _____

C Choose two soft skills from Exercise A. Give examples of why you are good at these skills.

_____

_____

_____

A Circle the answers.

1. Using less energy will help us to ____ the environment.   (a.) protect   b. reduce

2. We need to ____ our paper and glass.   a. recycle   b. protect

3. Everyone should take ____ for saving the earth.   a. energy   b. responsibility

4. New appliances are usually more ____ than older ones.   a. important   b. energy-efficient

5. The earth's temperature is increasing because of ____ warming.   a. electrical   b. global

6. Try to ____ energy use. Turn off your appliances.   a. cut down on   b. recycle

B Complete the text. Use the words from Exercise A.

Find Out More About Living Green

Do you want to p *rotect* _____ the environment? Not sure what to do?

Come to the Living Green informational talk to find out more. Learn about some

simple steps to c _____ energy use, including:

• how to buy e _____ appliances

• how to start a carpool club

• how to r _____ bottles, cans, and clothing

It's time to take responsibility for saving the earth from g _____

warming!

Gates Public Library, Thursday 6:00 p.m.–7:00 p.m. All welcome.

C Match the problems with the suggestions. Complete the chart.

| Carpool with co-workers. | Recycle your glass and paper. | Use energy-efficient appliances. |

Problem	**Advice**
1. I want to reduce my energy use.	*Use energy-efficient appliances.*
2. I want to cut down on driving.	
3. I want to cut down on trash.	

A Complete the sentences.

cut down on	energy-efficient	global	protect	recycle	responsibility

1. Using less energy will help us to _____*protect*_____ the environment.

2. We need to _____ our paper and glass.

3. Everyone should take _____ for saving the earth.

4. New appliances are usually more _____ than older ones.

5. The earth's temperature is increasing because of _____ warming.

6. Try to _____ energy use. Turn off your appliances.

B Complete the text. Use the words from Exercise A.

Find Out More About Living Green

Do you want to _____*protect*_____ the environment? Not sure what to do?

Come to the Living Green informational talk to find out more. Learn about some

simple steps to _____ energy use, including:

• how to buy _____ appliances

• how to start a carpool club

• how to _____ bottles, cans, and clothing

It's time to take _____ for saving the earth from

_____ warming!

Gates Public Library, Thursday 6:00 p.m.–7:00 p.m. All welcome.

C Match the problems with the suggestions. Write another problem and a suggestion.

Carpool with co-workers.	Recycle your glass and paper.	Use energy-efficient appliances.

Problem	Advice
1. I want to reduce my energy use.	*Use energy-efficient appliances.*
2. I want to cut down on driving.	
3. I want to cut down on trash.	
4.	

Lesson A Get ready

A Complete the sentences.

1. Using less energy will help us to p r o t e c t the environment.
2. We need to re __ __ __ __ __ our paper and glass.
3. Everyone should take r__ __ __ __ __ __ __ __ __ __ __ __ __y for saving the earth.
4. New appliances are usually more energy-e__ __ __ __ __ __ __t than older ones.
5. The earth's temperature is increasing because of g__ __ __ __ __ warming.
6. Try to c__ __   d__ __ __   __ __ energy use. Turn off your appliances.

B Complete the text. Use the words from Exercise A and the words in the box.

| carpool   earth   environment   informational |

Find Out More About Living Green

Do you want to _____ *protect* _____ the _____ ? Not sure

what to do? Come to the Living Green _____ talk to find out more.

Learn about some simple steps to _____ energy use, including:

• how to buy _____ appliances

• how to start a _____ club

• how to _____ bottles, cans, and clothing

It's time to take _____ for saving the _____

from _____ warming!

Gates Public Library, Thursday 6:00 p.m.–7:00 p.m. All welcome.

C Suggest advice for these problems. Add two more problems and suggestions.

Problem	Advice
1. I want to reduce my energy use.	*Use energy-efficient appliances.*
2. I want to cut down on driving.	
3. I want to cut down on trash.	
4.	
5.	

Lesson B Conditional sentences

A Circle the noun that goes with each verb.

1. reduce   a. your car   (b.) energy use

2. recycle   a. electricity   b. newspapers

3. tune up   a. water leaks   b. your car

4. save   a. gas   b. lightbulbs

5. fix   a. trees   b. water leaks

6. replace   a. lightbulbs   b. gas

B Match.

1. If everyone carpooled to work, __e__   a. I would save water.

2. Frank would save money on gas ____   b. if she replaced her lightbulbs.

3. If people recycled their paper, ____   c. if you used recycled paper.

4. You would cut down on trash ____   d. if he took the bus to work.

5. If I took shorter showers, ____   e. the roads would be less crowded.

6. Sasha would use less electricity ____   f. we would save trees.

C Circle the correct words.

1. If you **used** / **would use** less plastic, you **reduced** / **would reduce** trash.

2. If drivers **checked** / **would check** their tires more often, they
   saved / **would save** gas.

3. You **helped** / **would help** the environment if you **bought** / **would buy**
   less plastic.

4. People **saved** / **would save** electricity if they **replaced** / **would replace**
   their lightbulbs.

5. Jan **used** / **would use** less water if she **took** / **would take** shorter showers.

6. If everyone **picked up** / **would pick up** their trash, the beach
   was / **would be** cleaner.

D Complete the sentence with your own ideas.

1. I would save gas if I _carpooled to school_ .

2. I would save electricity if I _____ .

Lesson B *Conditional sentences*

A Circle two nouns that go with each verb.

1. reduce   a. your car   (b.) energy use   (c.) trash

2. recycle   a. electricity   b. newspapers   c. plastic

3. tune up   a. water leaks   b. your car   c. your engine

4. save   a. gas   b. water   c. lightbulbs

5. fix   a. trees   b. water leaks   c. your car

6. replace   a. lightbulbs   b. tires   c. gas

B Complete the first part of each sentence. Then match.

carpooled	cut	recycled	save	took	use

1. If everyone _carpooled_ to work, _e_   a. I would save water.

2. Frank would _____ money on gas ____   b. if she replaced her lightbulbs.

3. If people _____ their paper, ____   c. if you used recycled paper.

4. You would _____ down on trash ____   d. if he took the bus to work.

5. If I _____ shorter showers, ____   e. the roads would be less crowded.

6. Sasha would _____ less electricity ____   f. we would save trees.

C Complete the sentences. Use the present unreal conditional.

1. (use / reduce) If you _____used_____ less plastic, you _would reduce_ trash.

2. (check / save) If drivers _____ their tires more often, they _____ gas.

3. (help / buy) You _____ the environment if you _____ less plastic.

4. (save / replace) People _____ electricity if they _____ their lightbulbs.

5. (use / take) Jan _____ less water if she _____ shorter showers.

6. (pick up / be) If everyone _____ their trash, the beach _____ cleaner.

D Complete the sentences with your own ideas.

1. I would save gas if I _carpooled to school_ .

2. I would save electricity if I _____ .

3. I would save trees if I _____ .

Lesson B Conditional sentences

Name: _____

A Write two nouns to go with each verb.

1. reduce _____*trash*_____ _____*energy use*_____

2. recycle _____ _____

3. tune up _____ _____

4. save _____ _____

5. fix _____ _____

6. replace _____ _____

B Complete the first part of each sentence with the correct form of the verb. Then match.

| carpool | cut | recycle | save | take | use |

1. If everyone ____*carpooled*____ to work, __*e*__   a. I would save water.

2. Frank would _____ money on gas ____   b. if she replaced her lightbulbs.

3. If people _____ their paper, ____   c. if you used recycled paper.

4. You would _____ down on trash ____   d. if he took the bus to work.

5. If I _____ shorter showers, ____   e. the roads would be less crowded.

6. Sasha would _____ less electricity ____   f. we would save trees.

C Complete the sentences with the pairs of verbs. Use the present unreal conditional.

| check / save | help / buy | pick up / be | save / replace | use / reduce | use / take |

1. If you _____*used*_____ less plastic, you _____*would reduce*_____ trash.

2. If drivers _____ their tires more often, they _____ gas.

3. You _____ the environment if you _____ less plastic.

4. People _____ electricity if they _____ their lightbulbs.

5. Jan _____ less water if she _____ shorter showers.

6. If everyone _____ their trash, the beach _____ cleaner.

D Complete the sentences with your own ideas.

1. I would save gas _*if I carpooled to school*_ .

2. I would save electricity _____ .

3. I would save trees _____ .

☑️ ■ ■

A Complete the sentences.

| energy | grow | melting | population | rising |

Causes

1. The oceans are getting warmer.
2. People are cutting down trees.
3. We are using up gas and oil.
4. The sea level is _____ .
5. There is not enough rain.
6. The world _____ is growing.

Effects

The ice caps are ___*melting*___ .

Animals and birds have fewer places to live.

We will need other sources of _____ .

Islands are sinking.

People cannot _____ as much food.

Cities are getting larger.

B Write sentences using the information in Exercise A.

1. *The oceans are getting warmer* . As a result, *the ice caps are melting* _____ .
          cause   effect

2. Since _____ , _____ .
                  cause   effect

3. _____ . Consequently, _____ .
           cause   effect

4. _____ . As a result, _____ .
           cause   effect

5. Since _____ , _____ .
                  cause   effect

6. _____ . Consequently, _____ .
           cause   effect

C Circle the correct connector.

1. **As a result** / **Due to** global warming, some diseases can spread more easily.

2. The temperature of the earth is rising. **Due to** / **Consequently**, there are more storms and floods.

3. Weather patterns are changing. **As a result** / **Since** , there is too much rain in some areas and not enough in others.

4. **Since** / **Consequently** cities are getting bigger, more animals are losing their natural habitats.

Lesson C Connectors

A Match each cause with an effect.

Causes

1. The oceans are getting warmer. _b_
2. People are cutting down trees. ____
3. We are using up gas and oil. ____
4. The sea level is rising. ____
5. There is not enough rain. ____
6. The world population is growing. ____

Effects

a. Cities are getting larger.
b. The ice caps are melting.
c. We will need other sources of energy.
d. People cannot grow as much food.
e. Animals and birds have fewer places to live.
f. Islands are sinking.

B Write sentences using the information from Exercise A.

1. _The oceans are getting warmer_ . As a result, _the ice caps are melting_ .
2. Since _____ , _____ .
3. _____ . Consequently, _____ .
4. _____ . As a result, _____ .
5. Since _____ , _____ .
6. _____ . Consequently, _____ .

C Complete the sentences.

As a result	Consequently	Due to	Since

1. _____Due to_____ global warming, some diseases can spread more easily.

2. The temperature of the earth is rising. _____ , there are more storms and floods.

3. Weather patterns are changing. _____ , there is too much rain in some areas and not enough in others.

4. _____ cities are getting bigger, more animals are losing their natural habitats.

Lesson **C** *Connectors*

■ ■ ☑

A Complete the sentences. Then match each cause with an effect.

| energy | growing | melting | rising |

Causes

1. The oceans are getting warmer. _b_

2. People are cutting down trees. ____

3. We are using up gas and oil. ____

4. The sea level is _____ . ____

5. There is not enough rain. ____

6. The world population is _____ . ____

Effects

a. Cities are getting larger.

b. The ice caps are ___*melting*___ .

c. We will need other sources

   of _____ .

d. People cannot grow as much food.

e. Animals and birds have fewer places to live.

f. Islands are sinking.

B Write sentences using the information from Exercise A.

1. (As a result)

   The oceans are getting warmer . *As a result, the ice caps are melting* .

2. (Since)

   _____ , _____ .

3. (Consequently)

   _____ . _____ .

4. (As a result)

   _____ . _____ .

5. (Since)

   _____ , _____ .

6. (Consequently)

   _____ . _____ .

C Complete the sentences with the correct connectors.

1. _____*Due to*_____ global warming, some diseases can spread more easily.

2. The temperature of the earth is rising. _____ , there are more storms and floods.

3. Weather patterns are changing. _____ , there is too much rain in some areas and not enough in others.

4. _____ cities are getting bigger, more animals are losing their natural habitats.

Lesson **D** *Reading*

A Skim the story. Find the words. Then circle the correct definition for each word.

1. race   a. agreement   (b.) competition

2. replied   a. asked   b. answered

3. route   a. rule   b. a direction to travel

4. swiftly   a. quickly   b. slowly

5. peacefully   a. quietly   b. noisily

6. approach   a. get nearer   b. go past

B Read the story. Then answer the questions.

The Tortoise and the Hare

One day a hare saw a tortoise walking slowly down the road. The hare began to laugh at the tortoise. "You're so slow," he said. "I can run much faster than you!" "Let's have a race," the tortoise replied. "Then we'll see which one of us is faster." The hare, who thought he was the fastest of all the animals, accepted.

They agreed on a route and started the race. The hare ran swiftly ahead. He ran so far ahead of the tortoise that he could not see the tortoise anymore. He said to himself, "If I take a little nap here, I'll still win the race easily." So the hare sat under a tree and was soon sleeping peacefully.

The tortoise continued with the race. He wasn't fast, but step by step he slowly approached his goal. When the hare woke up, it was too late. The tortoise was already passing the finish line. The hare was furious. The tortoise had won! The tortoise had never stopped, and as a result he won the race.

1. Why did the hare laugh at the tortoise?

(a.) He was slow.   b. He was old.

2. What did they decide to do?

a. They decided to walk together.   b. They decided to have a race.

3. Why did the hare lose?

a. He took a nap.   b. He got lost.

4. Why did the tortoise win?

a. He continued slowly but surely.   b. He took a shorter route.

C Circle the moral (meaning) of the story.

a. The fastest is not always the winner.   b. Don't give up too soon.

A Skim the story. Find the words. Then circle the correct definition for each word.

1. race   a. agreement   (b.) competition   c. communication

2. replied   a. asked   b. answered   c. complained

3. route   a. rule   b. a direction to travel   c. a part of a plant

4. swiftly   a. quickly   b. slowly   c. carefully

5. peacefully   a. quietly   b. noisily   c. angrily

6. approach   a. get nearer   b. go past   c. forget about

B Read the story. Then match the questions and the answers.

The Tortoise and the Hare

One day a hare saw a tortoise walking slowly down the road. The hare began to laugh at the tortoise. "You're so slow," he said. "I can run much faster than you!" "Let's have a race," the tortoise replied. "Then we'll see which one of us is faster." The hare, who thought he was the fastest of all the animals, accepted.

They agreed on a route and started the race. The hare ran swiftly ahead. He ran so far ahead of the tortoise that he could not see the tortoise anymore. He said to himself, "If I take a little nap here, I'll still win the race easily." So the hare sat under a tree and was soon sleeping peacefully.

The tortoise continued with the race. He wasn't fast, but step by step he slowly approached his goal. When the hare woke up, it was too late. The tortoise was already passing the finish line. The hare was furious. The tortoise had won! The tortoise had never stopped, and as a result he won the race.

1. Why did the hare laugh at the tortoise? __*d*__   a. They decided to have a race.

2. What did they decide to do? _____   b. He continued slowly but surely.

3. Why did the hare lose? _____   c. He took a nap.

4. Why did the tortoise win? _____   d. He was slow.

C Circle the moral (meaning) of the story.

a. The fastest is not always the winner.

b. Don't give up too soon.

c. He who laughs, loses.

A Skim the story. Find the words. Then match each word with the correct definition.

1. race __c__   a. get nearer

2. replied ____   b. quietly

3. route ____   c. competition

4. swiftly ____   d. answered

5. peacefully ____   e. a direction to travel

6. approach ____   f. quickly

B Read the story. Then answer the questions.

The Tortoise and the Hare

One day a hare saw a tortoise walking slowly down the road. The hare began to laugh at the tortoise. "You're so slow," he said. "I can run much faster than you!" "Let's have a race," the tortoise replied. "Then we'll see which one of us is faster." The hare, who thought he was the fastest of all the animals, accepted.

They agreed on a route and started the race. The hare ran swiftly ahead. He ran so far ahead of the tortoise that he could not see the tortoise anymore. He said to himself, "If I take a little nap here, I'll still win the race easily." So the hare sat under a tree and was soon sleeping peacefully.

The tortoise continued with the race. He wasn't fast, but step by step he slowly approached his goal. When the hare woke up, it was too late. The tortoise was already passing the finish line. The hare was furious. The tortoise had won! The tortoise had never stopped, and as a result he won the race.

1. Why did the hare laugh at the tortoise? _He was slow._____

2. What did they decide to do? _____

3. Why did the hare lose? _____

4. Why did the tortoise win? _____

C Write the moral (meaning) of the story in your own words.

_____

A Complete the chart.

easy to carry	free	prefer	reuse	trash

The Causes and Effects of Too Many Plastic Bags

Causes	Effects
1. Plastic bags are light and _easy to carry_ .	Customers ____*prefer*____ them.
2. Stores give away plastic bags for _____ .	Customers don't _____ them.
3. Customers throw the plastic bags away.	There are too many bags in the _____ .
4. There is a huge amount of plastic in the ground.	Chemicals get into the soil and the water.

B Use the sentences above to complete the paragraph.

The Causes and Effects of Too Many Plastic Bags

We use too many plastic bags, and it is a serious environmental problem. One cause is that plastic bags are light and easy to carry. As a result, customers ___*prefer*___ them. Another cause is that stores give away plastic bags _____ _____ . Consequently, customers don't _____ _____ . Since customers throw the plastic bags away, there are too many bags in the _____ . Due to the huge _____ of _____ in the ground, chemicals get into the soil and the _____ . If we used fewer plastic bags, we would cause less damage to the environment.

C Choose one of the problems. Complete the chart.

Not enough clean water.	Not enough trees.	Too much air pollution.

Problem: _____

Causes	Effects

A Complete the chart.

| easy to carry | free | prefer | reuse | throw | trash |

The Causes and Effects of Too Many Plastic Bags

Causes	Effects
1. Plastic bags are light and *easy to carry* .	Customers _____ them.
2. Stores give away plastic bags for _____ .	Customers don't _____ them.
3. Customers _____ the plastic bags away.	There are too many bags in the _____ .
4. There is a huge amount of plastic in the ground.	Chemicals get into the soil and the water.

B Use the sentences above to complete the paragraph.

> # The Causes and Effects of Too Many Plastic Bags
>
> We use too many plastic bags, and it is a serious environmental problem. One cause is that plastic bags are light and easy to carry. As a result, customers *prefer them* _____ . Another cause is that stores give away plastic bags _____ . Consequently, customers don't _____ . Since customers throw the plastic bags away, there are too many bags _____ . Due to the huge _____ in the ground, chemicals get into the soil and the water. If we used fewer plastic bags, we would cause less damage to the environment.

C Choose one of the problems. Complete the chart.

| Not enough clean water. | Not enough trees. | Too much air pollution. |

Problem: _____

Causes	Effects

Unit 9 Daily living

Lesson **E** *Writing*

Name: _____

A Match the causes with the effects.

The Causes and Effects of Too Many Plastic Bags

Causes	Effects
1. Plastic bags are light and easy to carry. __*d*__	a. There are too many bags in the trash.
2. Stores give away plastic bags for free. _____	b. Customers prefer them.
3. Customers throw the plastic bags away. _____	c. Chemicals get into the soil and the water.
4. There is a huge amount of plastic in the ground. _____	d. Customers don't reuse them.

B Use the sentences above to complete the paragraph.

The Causes and Effects of Too Many Plastic Bags

We use too many plastic bags, and it is a serious environmental problem. One cause is that plastic bags *are light and easy to carry* . As a result, customers prefer them. Another cause is that stores _____ . Consequently, customers don't _____ . Since customers _____ , there are _____ . Due to the _____ in the ground, chemicals get into _____ . If we used fewer plastic bags, we would cause less damage to the environment.

C Choose one of the problems or use your own idea. Complete the chart.

Not enough clean water.   Not enough trees.   Too much air pollution.

Problem: _____

Causes	Effects

A Read the clues. Complete the crossword puzzle.

| efficient | energy | environmental | global | pollution | recycle |

Down

1. These new lightbulbs are more energy-_____ .

2. Cars are one cause of air _____ .

3. The earth's temperature is rising. This is called _____ warming.

4. Using less air-conditioning will reduce our _____ use.

5. Don't throw your bottles in the trash. You should _____ them.

Across

6. The melting ice caps are a serious _____ problem.

B Complete the chart with ways to save energy, gas, and water.

Carpool to work.	Take shorter showers.
Don't use air-conditioning.	Turn down your heater.
Share a car with your neighbor.	Use the dishwasher only when it is full.

Save energy at home	Save gas	Save water
Don't use air-conditioning.	Carpool to work.	

A Read the clues. Complete the crossword puzzle.

```
        ¹e                        ²p
         f        ³g
    ⁴e   f              ⁵r
⁶e       i
         c
         i
         e
         n
         t
```

Down

1. These new lightbulbs are more energy-_____ .
2. Cars are one cause of air _____ .
3. The earth's temperature is rising. This is called _____ warming.
4. Using less air-conditioning will reduce our _____ use.
5. Don't throw your bottles in the trash. You should _____ them.

Across

6. The melting ice caps are a serious _____ problem.

B Complete the chart with ways to save energy, gas, and water.

Carpool to work.	Take the bus or the train.
Don't leave water running.	Turn down your heater.
Don't use air-conditioning.	Use energy-efficient lightbulbs.
Share a car with your neighbor.	Use the dishwasher only when it is full.
Take shorter showers.	

Save energy at home	Save gas	Save water	
	Carpool to work.		

Lesson F *Another view*

A Read the clues. Complete the crossword puzzle.

Down

1. These new lightbulbs are more energy-_____ .
2. Cars are one cause of air _____ .
3. The earth's temperature is rising. This is called _____ warming.
4. Using less air-conditioning will reduce our _____ use.
5. Don't throw your bottles in the trash. You should _____ them.

Across

6. The melting ice caps are a serious _____ problem.

B Complete the chart with ways to save energy, gas, and water.

Carpool to work.	Take shorter showers.
Don't leave water running.	Take the bus or the train.
Don't use air-conditioning.	Turn down your heater.
Don't water your grass.	Turn out the lights.
Ride a bicycle.	Use energy-efficient lightbulbs.
Share a car with your neighbor.	Use the dishwasher only when it is full.

Save energy at home	Save gas	Save water
	Carpool to work.	

Lesson A *Get ready*

☑ ■ ■

A Circle the correct word.

1. Throwing rice at a wedding is an American (tradition)/ reception.

2. The color red **prevents** / **symbolizes** good luck in Vietnam.

3. The wedding couple doesn't always invite **acquaintances** / **parents** to the ceremony.

4. After a wedding ceremony, there is usually a **concert** / **reception**.

5. The dinner sometimes has several **parties** / **courses**.

6. I am looking **forward** / **excited** to my sister's wedding next year.

B Read the quiz. Circle *T* (True) or *F* (False).

What do you know about wedding customs in Vietnam?

1. The guests throw rice at the newly married couple.	T	(F)
2. The color red symbolizes good fortune.	T	F
3. Traditionally, only family members are invited to the wedding ceremony.	T	F
4. The party usually includes a dinner with four courses.	T	F
5. It is a tradition that guests give money to the bride and groom.	T	F
6. The bride and groom are usually registered for gifts at a store.	T	F

C Complete the chart with information about wedding customs in your culture.

Location of ceremony	
Reception	
Food courses	

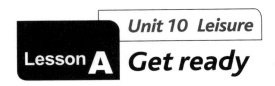

A Complete the sentences.

acquaintances	courses	forward	reception	symbolizes	tradition

1. Throwing rice at a wedding is an American _____*tradition*_____ .

2. The color red _____ good luck in Vietnam.

3. The wedding couple doesn't always invite _____ to the ceremony.

4. After a wedding ceremony, there is usually a _____ .

5. The dinner sometimes has several _____ .

6. I am looking _____ to my sister's wedding next year.

B Complete the sentences in the quiz. Then circle *T* (True) or *F* (False).

ceremony	courses	registered	symbolizes	throw	tradition

What do you know about wedding customs in Vietnam?

1. The guests _____*throw*_____ rice at the newly married couple.   T (F)

2. The color red _____ good fortune.   T F

3. Traditionally, only family members are invited to the wedding

   _____ .   T F

4. The party usually includes a dinner with four _____ .   T F

5. It is a _____ that guests give money to the bride and groom.   T F

6. The bride and groom are usually _____ for gifts at a store.   T F

C Complete the chart with information about wedding customs in your culture.

Location of ceremony	
Reception	
Food courses	
Something that symbolizes good fortune	

A Complete the sentences.

1. Throwing rice at a wedding is an American tr _a_ _d_ _i_ _t_ _i_ _o_ _n_.

2. The color red sy __ __ __ __ __ __ __ __ s good luck in Vietnam.

3. The wedding couple doesn't always invite

   ac __ __ __ __ __ __ __ __ __ __ __ s to the ceremony.

4. After a wedding ceremony, there is usually a re __ __ __ __ __ __ n.

5. The dinner sometimes has several co __ __ __ __ s.

6. I am looking fo __ __ __ __ d to my sister's wedding next year.

B Complete the sentences in the quiz. Then circle *T* (True) or *F* (False).

ceremony	fortune	registered	tradition
courses	invited	throw	

What do you know about wedding customs in Vietnam?

1. The guests _____*throw*_____ rice at the newly married couple. T ⒡

2. The color red symbolizes good _____ . T F

3. Traditionally, only family members are _____ to the wedding T F
   _____ .

4. The party usually includes a dinner with four _____ . T F

5. It is a _____ that guests give money to the bride and groom. T F

6. The bride and groom are usually _____ for gifts at a store. T F

C Complete the chart with information about wedding customs in your culture.

Location of ceremony	
Reception	
Food courses	
Something that symbolizes good fortune	
Gifts	

Lesson B Conditional sentences

☑ ■ ■

A Circle the answers.

1. If I go shopping tomorrow, _____ .

    (a.) I'll spend too much money   b. I would spend too much money

2. If Sue had more free time, _____ .

    a. she will listen to music more often   b. she would listen to music more often

3. They won't eat dinner outside _____ .

    a. if the weather is cold   b. if the weather were cold

4. We would invite all our friends over _____ .

    a. if our house were bigger   b. if our house is bigger

5. If you didn't stay up so late, _____ .

    a. you won't feel so tired   b. you wouldn't feel so tired

6. I'll wear my new shirt _____ .

    a. if I go to the party   b. if I would go to the party

B Circle the correct words.

1. Denise is spending New Year's Eve in Florida. If the weather **is** / **will be**
   warm, she **goes** / **will go** to the beach. If she **stays** / **stayed** home, she
   will make / **would make** dinner with friends.

2. Jian and Ling are spending New Year's Eve in Sydney, Australia. If they
   watch / **will watch** the fireworks, they **stay out** / **will stay out** until the
   next morning. If they **were** / **would be** at home in Seattle, they **go** / **would go**
   to bed at midnight.

3. We are spending New Year's Eve at our parents' house. If our friends
   come over / **will come over**, we **go** / **will go** to a club later in the evening. If
   we **weren't** / **wouldn't be** at our parents' house, we **invited** / **would invite** all
   our friends over for a party.

C Complete the sentences.

1. If I weren't at school right now, I _____ .

2. If I spend time with friends or family tonight, I _____ .

Lesson B *Conditional sentences*

A Match.

1. If I go shopping tomorrow, __e__
2. If Sue had more free time, ____
3. They won't eat dinner outside ____
4. We would invite all our friends over ____
5. If you didn't stay up so late, ____
6. I'll wear my new shirt ____

a. if the weather is cold.
b. you wouldn't feel so tired.
c. if our house were bigger.
d. if I go to the party.
e. I'll spend too much money.
f. she would listen to music more often.

B Circle the correct words.

1. Denise is spending New Year's Eve in Florida. If the weather **is** / **will be** warm, she **goes** / **will go** to the beach. If she **stays** / **stayed** home, she **will make** / **would make** dinner with friends.

2. Jian and Ling are spending New Year's Eve in Sydney, Australia. If they **watch** / **will watch** the fireworks, they **stay out** / **will stay out** until the next morning. If they **were** / **would be** at home in Seattle, they **go** / **would go** to bed at midnight.

3. We are spending New Year's Eve at our parents' house. If our friends **come over** / **will come over**, we **go** / **will go** to a club later in the evening. If we **weren't** / **wouldn't be** at our parents' house, we **invited** / **would invite** all our friends over for a party.

4. I am spending New Year's Eve in Boston. If the weather **isn't** / **won't be** too cold, I **walk** / **will walk** to a bar to listen to live music. If I **didn't live** / **wouldn't live** in the center of Boston, I **will have** / **would have** to drive to the bar.

C Answer the questions.

1. If you weren't at school right now, where would you be?

_____

2. If you spend time with friends or family tonight, what will you do?

_____

Lesson B *Conditional sentences*

A Complete the sentences. Then match.

eat	go	had	invite	stay	wear

1. If I _____*go*_____ shopping tomorrow, __*e*__   a. if the weather is cold.

2. If Sue _____ more free time, ____   b. you wouldn't feel so tired.

3. They won't _____ dinner outside ____   c. if our house were bigger.

4. We would _____ all our friends over ____   d. if I go to the party.

5. If you didn't _____ up so late, ____   e. I'll spend too much money.

6. I'll _____ my new shirt ____   f. she would listen to music more often.

B Complete the sentences. Use the real future or unreal conditional forms
of the verbs.

1. Denise is spending New Year's Eve in Florida. If the weather _____*is*_____
   (be)

   warm, she _____*will go*_____ to the beach. If she _____ home,
   (go)   (stay)

   she _____ dinner with friends.
   (make)

2. Jian and Ling are spending New Year's Eve in Sydney, Australia. If

   they _____ the fireworks, they _____ until
   (watch)   (stay out)

   the next morning. If they _____ at home in Seattle, they
   (be)

   _____ to bed at midnight.
   (go)

3. We are spending New Year's Eve at our parents' house. If our friends

   _____ , we _____ to a club later in the evening. If
   (come over)   (go)

   we _____ at our parents' house, we _____ all our
   (be)   (invite)

   friends over for a party.

4. I am spending New Year's Eve in Boston. If the weather _____
   (not be)

   too cold, I _____ to a bar to listen to live music. If I _____
   (walk)   (not live)

   in the center of Boston, I _____ to drive to the bar.
   (have)

C Answer the questions. Use the back of this paper.

1. If you weren't at school right now, where would you be?

2. If you spend time with friends or family tonight, what will you do?

 **Lesson C** *Expressing hopes and wishes*

A Circle the correct words.

1. Ronnie hopes his son **comes** / **came** home for Thanksgiving.

2. Elena wishes her friends **call** / **would call** her more often.

3. Francisco hopes his parents **will buy** / **bought** him a cell phone for his birthday.

4. Tam wishes he **can buy** / **could buy** a new car.

5. Katrina hopes her mother **will bake** / **baked** some cookies next weekend.

6. Maya and Alex wish they **can take** / **could take** a vacation.

B Correct the mistake in each sentence. Each mistake is <u>underlined</u>.

1. We hope all our friends <u>would</u> *will* come to our wedding party.

2. Frank and Ella hope their children <u>visited</u> them this weekend.

3. Pamela hopes her boyfriend <u>would</u> take her out for dinner.

4. My sister wishes she <u>has</u> a bigger house.

5. Marta and Juan wish their parents <u>visit</u> them in the United States.

6. My wife wishes I <u>will</u> give her flowers more often.

C Write three things you hope or wish for in the Wish Tree.

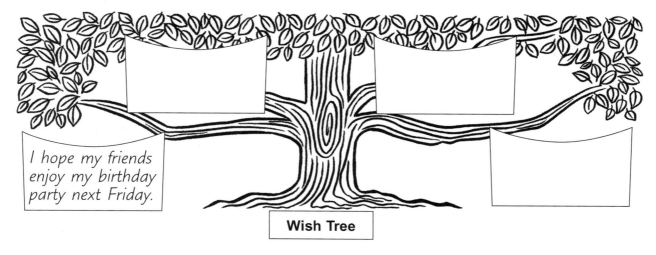

I hope my friends enjoy my birthday party next Friday.

Wish Tree

Lesson C *Expressing hopes and wishes*

A Complete the sentences.

1. Ronnie hopes his son *will come / comes* home for Thanksgiving.
   (come)

2. Elena wishes her friends _____ her more often.
   (call)

3. Francisco hopes his parents _____ him a cell phone for his birthday.
   (buy)

4. Tam wishes he _____ a new car.
   (buy)

5. Katrina hopes her mother _____ some cookies next weekend.
   (bake)

6. Maya and Alex wish they _____ a vacation.
   (take)

B Correct the mistake in each sentence.

1. We hope all our friends ~~would~~ *will* come to our wedding party.

2. Frank and Ella hope their children visited them this weekend.

3. Pamela hopes her boyfriend would take her out for dinner.

4. My sister wishes she has a bigger house.

5. Marta and Juan wish their parents visit them in the United States.

6. My wife wishes I will give her flowers more often.

C Write four things you hope or wish for in the Wish Tree.

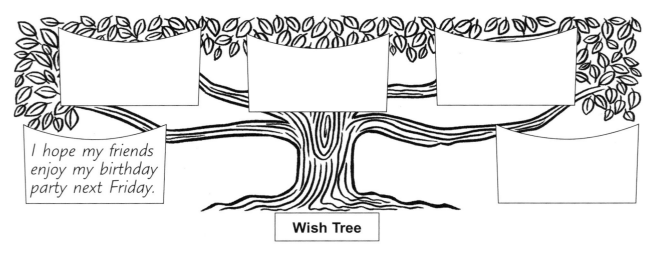

I hope my friends enjoy my birthday party next Friday.

Wish Tree

Lesson **C** Expressing hopes and wishes

A Write sentences.

1. Ronnie / hope / his son / come home for Thanksgiving

   Ronnie hopes his son will come home for Thanksgiving.

2. Elena / wish / her friends / call her more often

   _____

3. Francisco / hope / his parents / buy him a cell phone for his birthday

   _____

4. Tam / wish / he / can buy a new car

   _____

5. Katrina / hope / her mother / bake some cookies next weekend

   _____

6. Maya and Alex / wish / they / can take a vacation

   _____

B Correct the mistakes. There are two mistakes in each sentence.

1. We ~~hopes~~ *hope* all our friends ~~would~~ *will* come to our wedding party.

2. Frank and Ella hopes their children visited them this weekend.

3. Pamela hope her boyfriend would take her out for dinner.

4. My sister wish she has a bigger house.

5. Marta and Juan wishes their parents visit them in the United States.

6. My wife wish I will give her flowers more often.

C Write five things you hope or wish for in the Wish Tree.

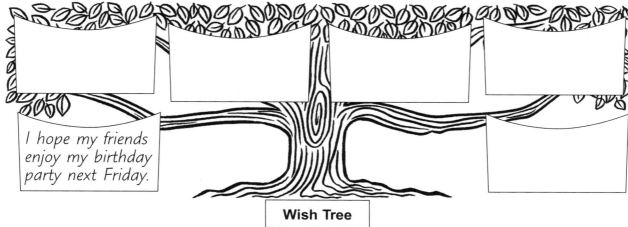

I hope my friends enjoy my birthday party next Friday.

Wish Tree

A Skim the article. Find the words in *italics*. Then circle the correct definition for each word.

1. branches   (a.) pieces of a tree   b. leaves
2. sticky   a. smooth   b. stays together
3. shows   a. concerts   b. instruments
4. cast   a. hide   b. throw
5. offered   a. given   b. asked for

B Read the article. Then circle the correct answers.

New Year's Eve Customs Around the World

In many cultures, New Year's Eve is an important time to celebrate the transition from the old year to the new one.

In Japan, people clean their houses and decorate them with pine and bamboo *branches*. They prepare many kinds of special New Year foods, such as *sticky* rice cakes. Businesses have end-of-year parties – bonenkai – for their employees. People write New Year cards that are delivered on January 1. At midnight, people hear a temple bell that rings 108 times.

In Rio de Janeiro, Brazil, millions of people go to the beaches to celebrate New Year's Eve. There are beach parties with fireworks at midnight. You can see live music *shows*, and hotels and restaurants offer special menus. In addition, Brazilians also offer gifts – flowers, perfume, or rice – to the Goddess of the Water. The gifts are placed into little boats, and then people *cast* them into the sea. People hope the goddess will give them good luck in the New Year.

In Scotland, people celebrate New Year's Eve with street parties and fireworks. People gather around the fire and sing a traditional song, "Auld Lang Syne." After midnight, neighbors visit each other. They bring traditional gifts, such as fruitcake. The visitor is *offered* a small glass of whiskey. The first visitor to enter a house in the New Year, the "first footing," could bring luck for the New Year.

---

1. What is a New Year food in Japan?   (a.) sticky rice cakes   b. fruit cakes
2. What is a "bonenkai"?   a. a party   b. a song
3. What do people hear at midnight in Japan?   a. a temple bell   b. fireworks
4. What gifts do Brazilians give to the water goddess?   a. flowers   b. fireworks
5. What is the "first footing"?   a. a visitor   b. a dance
6. What do people in Scotland offer to their visitors?   a. flowers   b. a glass of whiskey
7. What is "Auld Lang Syne"?   a. a decoration   b. a song

Lesson D *Reading*

A Skim the article. Find the words in *italics*. Then match each word with the correct definition.

1. branches __c__   a. given
2. sticky _____   b. throw
3. shows _____   c. pieces of a tree
4. cast _____   d. stays together
5. offered _____   e. concerts

B Read the article. Then answer the questions.

New Year's Eve Customs Around the World

In many cultures, New Year's Eve is an important time to celebrate the transition from the old year to the new one.

In Japan, people clean their houses and decorate them with pine and bamboo *branches*. They prepare many kinds of special New Year foods, such as *sticky* rice cakes. Businesses have end-of-year parties – bonenkai – for their employees. People write New Year cards that are delivered on January 1. At midnight, people hear a temple bell that rings 108 times.

In Rio de Janeiro, Brazil, millions of people go to the beaches to celebrate New Year's Eve. There are beach parties with fireworks at midnight. You can see live music *shows*, and hotels and restaurants offer special menus. In addition, Brazilians also offer gifts – flowers, perfume, or rice – to the Goddess of the Water. The gifts are placed into little boats, and then people *cast* them into the sea. People hope the goddess will give them good luck in the New Year.

In Scotland, people celebrate New Year's Eve with street parties and fireworks. People gather around the fire and sing a traditional song, "Auld Lang Syne." After midnight, neighbors visit each other. They bring traditional gifts, such as fruitcake. The visitor is *offered* a small glass of whiskey. The first visitor to enter a house in the New Year, the "first footing," could bring luck for the New Year.

1. What is a New Year food in Japan? _Sticky rice cakes._____

2. What is a "bonenkai"? _____

3. What do people hear at midnight in Japan? _____

4. What gifts do Brazilians give to the water goddess? _____

5. What is the "first footing"? _____

6. What do people in Scotland offer to their visitors? _____

7. What is "Auld Lang Syne"? _____

A Skim the article. Find words with these definitions. Write the words.

1. pieces of a tree: b *ranches*

2. stays together: s_____

3. concerts: s_____

4. throw: c_____

5. given: o_____

B Read the article. Then write questions.

New Year's Eve Customs Around the World

In many cultures, New Year's Eve is an important time to celebrate the transition from the old year to the new one.

In Japan, people clean their houses and decorate them with pine and bamboo *branches*. They prepare many kinds of special New Year foods, such as *sticky* rice cakes. Businesses have end-of-year parties – bonenkai – for their employees. People write New Year cards that are delivered on January 1. At midnight, people hear a temple bell that rings 108 times.

In Rio de Janeiro, Brazil, millions of people go to the beaches to celebrate New Year's Eve. There are beach parties with fireworks at midnight. You can see live music *shows*, and hotels and restaurants offer special menus. In addition, Brazilians also offer gifts – flowers, perfume, or rice – to the Goddess of the Water. The gifts are placed into little boats, and then people *cast* them into the sea. People hope the goddess will give them good luck in the New Year.

In Scotland, people celebrate New Year's Eve with street parties and fireworks. People gather around the fire and sing a traditional song, "Auld Lang Syne." After midnight, neighbors visit each other. They bring traditional gifts, such as fruitcake. The visitor is *offered* a small glass of whiskey. The first visitor to enter a house in the New Year, the "first footing," could bring luck for the New Year.

1. *What is a New Year food in Japan?* Sticky rice cakes.

2. _____ It's an end-of-year party in Japan.

3. _____ They hear a temple bell.

4. _____ Flowers, perfume, or rice.

5. _____ It's the first visitor to enter a house in the New Year.

6. _____ They offer a small glass of whiskey.

7. _____ It's the name of a traditional song in Scotland.

A Label the sentences: *A* (topic sentence), *B* (meanings or symbolism), *C* (customs), or *D* (conclusion).

The Fourth of July

_____ In the morning, we usually see a parade in the neighborhood streets.

_C_ It is also a day when friends and family get together.

_____ People celebrate winning independence from Great Britain.

_____ At night, there is a big fireworks show with music.

_A_ My favorite celebration is the Fourth of July.

_D_ I like the Fourth of July because it is a summer celebration that lasts all day.

_____ For lunch, we usually have a barbecue or picnic in the park.

_____ We decorate our homes with the American flag.

_____ This holiday is also known as Independence Day.

B Rewrite the sentences in Exercise A as a paragraph.

My Favorite Celebration

My favorite celebration is the Fourth of July. _____

_____

_____

_____

_____

_____

C Internet task: Go on the Internet. Look up one of the holidays. Complete the chart. If you don't have access to the Internet, ask a partner about a holiday in his or her country.

| Inti Raymi   Mardi Gras |

Holiday: _____

Where	When	Why	Customs

A Label the sentences: *A* (topic sentence), *B* (meanings or symbolism), *C* (customs), or *D* (conclusion).

The Fourth of July

_____ In the morning, we usually see a parade in the neighborhood streets.

_____ It is also a day when friends and family get together.

_____ People celebrate winning independence from Great Britain.

_____ At night, there is a big fireworks show with music.

_A_ My favorite celebration is the Fourth of July.

_____ I like the Fourth of July because it is a summer celebration that lasts all day.

_____ For lunch, we usually have a barbecue or picnic in the park.

_____ We decorate our homes with the American flag.

_____ This holiday is also known as Independence Day.

B Rewrite the sentences in Exercise A as a paragraph.

My Favorite Celebration

My favorite celebration is the Fourth of July. _____

_____

_____

_____

_____

_____

C Internet task: Go on the Internet. Look up one of the holidays. Complete the chart. If you don't have access to the Internet, ask a partner about a holiday in his or her country.

| Inti Raymi | Mardi Gras | Obon |

Holiday: _____

Where	When	Why	Customs

A Match. Then label the sentences: *A* (topic sentence), *B* (meanings or symbolism), *C* (customs), or *D* (conclusion).

The Fourth of July

_____ In the morning, we usually see _____	a. have a barbecue or picnic in the park.
_____ It is also a day when _____	b. a parade in the neighborhood streets.
_____ People celebrate winning _____	c. friends and family get together.
_____ At night, there is _____	d. a big fireworks show with music.
_A_ My favorite celebration _f_	e. independence from Great Britain.
_____ I like the Fourth of July because _____	f. is the Fourth of July.
_____ For lunch, we usually _____	g. with the American flag.
_____ We decorate our homes _____	h. it is a summer celebration that lasts all day.
_____ This holiday is also known as _____	i. Independence Day.

B Rewrite the sentences in Exercise A as a paragraph.

My Favorite Celebration

My favorite celebration is the Fourth of July.
_____

_____

_____

_____

_____

C Internet task: Go on the Internet. Look up one of the holidays. Complete the chart. If you don't have access to the Internet, ask a partner about a holiday in his or her country.

| Inti Raymi | Mardi Gras | Obon | Songkran |

Holiday: _____

Where	When	Why	Customs

Name: _____

A How much do you know about U.S. holidays? Circle the correct answers.

Holiday Quiz

1. When is New Year's Eve?
ⓐ December 31   b. January 1   c. January 31

2. When is Independence Day?
a. July 1   b. July 4   c. July 5

3. What is the traditional food on Thanksgiving?
a. beef   b. turkey   c. eggs

4. What do people usually do on Valentine's Day?
a. give flowers and chocolates to someone they love
b. wear green hats   c. sing a song

5. When is April Fools' Day?
a. April 10   b. April 21   c. April 1

B Complete the recipe for chocolate brownies. (Then try to bake some at home!)

Ingredients

²/₃ cup flour
½ teaspoon baking powder
¼ teaspoon salt
⅓ cup butter
2 squares (1 ounce each) chocolate

1 cup sugar
2 eggs, beaten
½ cup chopped nuts
1 teaspoon vanilla

| add | beat | melt | pour | preheat | serve |

1. __*Preheat*__ the oven to 350°F. Mix the flour, baking powder, and salt in a bowl.

2. _____ the butter and chocolate over hot water or very low heat.

3. In a second bowl, _____ the eggs. _____ the sugar to the eggs a little at a time.

4. Mix in the chocolate and butter mixture. Stir in the flour mixture and blend well.

5. Stir in chopped nuts and vanilla.

6. _____ into an 8-inch square pan. Bake at 350° for about 25 minutes.

7. Cool in the pan and cut into squares. _____ with ice cream.

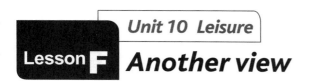
Lesson F **Another view**

Name: _____

A How much do you know about U.S. holidays? Write the answers.

Holiday Quiz

1. When is New Year's Eve?

_____December 31_____

2. When is Independence Day?

_____

3. What is the traditional food on Thanksgiving?

_____

4. What do people usually do on Valentine's Day?

_____

5. When is April Fools' Day?

_____

B Read the recipe for chocolate brownies. Number the steps in the correct order.
(Then try to bake some at home!)

Ingredients

²/₃ cup flour	1 cup sugar
¹/₂ teaspoon baking powder	2 eggs, beaten
¹/₄ teaspoon salt	¹/₂ cup chopped nuts
¹/₃ cup butter	1 teaspoon vanilla
2 squares (1 ounce each) chocolate	

_____ Cool in the pan and cut into squares. Serve with ice cream.

_____ In a second bowl, beat the eggs. Add the sugar to the eggs a little at a time.

_____ Melt the butter and chocolate over hot water or very low heat.

__4__ Mix in the chocolate and butter mixture. Stir in the flour mixture and blend well.

_____ Pour into an 8-inch square pan. Bake at 350° for about 25 minutes.

__1__ Preheat the oven to 350°F. Mix the flour, baking powder, and salt in a bowl.

_____ Stir in chopped nuts and vanilla.

A How much do you know about U.S. holidays? Write questions.

Holiday Quiz

1. *When is New Year's Eve?* _____
   It is December 31.

2. _____
   It is July 4.

3. _____
   Turkey.

4. _____
   They give flowers and chocolates to someone they love.

5. _____
   It is April 1.

B Read the recipe for chocolate brownies. Number the steps in the correct order.
(Then try to bake some at home!)

Ingredients		
²/₃ cup flour	1 cup sugar	
1/2 teaspoon baking powder	2 eggs, beaten	
1/4 teaspoon salt	1/2 cup chopped nuts	
1/3 cup butter	1 teaspoon vanilla	
2 squares (1 ounce each) chocolate		

_____ Cool in the pan and cut into squares. Serve with ice cream.

_____ In a second bowl, beat the eggs. Add the sugar to the eggs a little at a time.

_____ Melt the butter and chocolate over hot water or very low heat.

_____ Mix in the chocolate and butter mixture. Stir in the flour mixture and blend well.

_____ Pour into an 8-inch square pan. Bake at 350° for about 25 minutes.

_1_ Preheat the oven to 350°F. Mix the flour, baking powder, and salt in a bowl.

_____ Stir in chopped nuts and vanilla.

Unit 1: Personal information

Lesson A: Get ready pages 1–3

A

1. Peter is good at solving problems. He is mathematical.
2. Gino is good at singing. He is musical.
3. Jasmin won a poetry contest. She is gifted in language.
4. Andy is good at fixing up cars. He is mechanical.
5. Jan is good at making delicious dinners. He has an aptitude for cooking.
6. Olga is good at everything. She's very bright.

B

Pete: Hi, Frankie. How's everything? You look depressed.
Frankie: Hi, Pete. Yeah, I got an F on my math test. I'm not very mathematical.
Pete: I'm terrible at math, too. I'm more gifted in language. What about you?
Frankie: I'm a mechanical person. I like finding out how machines work and fixing them.
Pete: Wow! Can you fix up my car?
Frankie: OK! Can you help me with my English homework?
Pete: Sure! No problem.

C

1. Count numbers and solve problems.
2. Fix up cars and make things.
3. Play an instrument and sing.

D

Answers will vary.

Lesson B: Noun clauses
pages 4–6

A

1. Do you think that computer skills are important for everyone?
2. Do people believe that science is more important than art?
3. Do you suppose that you need mechanical skills to fix up a car?
4. Do you believe that everyone has some musical skills?
5. Do you feel that it is important to learn grammar?
6. Do you think that more education helps people get better jobs?

B

1. Jean thinks that Aimee is good at singing.
2. Do you believe that mathematical skills are important?
3. Everyone knows that education is important.
4. Do you think that I am good at dancing?
5. Frank realizes that he has an aptitude for science.

C

Answers will vary.

Lesson C: Parts of speech
pages 7–9

A

1. skillfully
2. easily
3. badly
4. good
5. fast
6. clear
7. perfectly
8. beautiful
9. Answers will vary.
10. Answers will vary.

B

1. We played very badly in the soccer game, and we lost.
2. Joe got 100 percent on the test because it was very easy.
3. My brother is a very slow driver.
4. Sharon talks very quickly, and I can't always understand her.
5. Daniela never makes mistakes. She checks her work very carefully.

6. Henrietta lived in France for many years, and she speaks French perfectly.

C

Answers will vary.

Lesson D: Reading pages 10–12

A

1. verbal: good with words
2. logical: good at solving puzzles
3. musical: gifted in singing or playing an instrument
4. visual: good at seeing or drawing pictures
5. kinesthetic: likes to move around
6. interpersonal: good at communicating
7. intrapersonal: understands their own feelings
8. naturalist: skillful with plants and animals

B

(b) what you are good at and enjoy

C

1. verbal
2. interpersonal
3. logical
4. visual
5. musical
6. intrapersonal
7. naturalist
8. kinesthetic

D

Answers will vary.

Lesson E: Writing pages 13–15

A

1. 3, 7, 8, 11, 13
2. 2, 6, 9, 10, 15
3. 1, 4, 5, 12, 14

B

Answers will vary.

C

Answers will vary.

Lesson F: Another view
pages 16–18

A

1. verbal, visual, logical

2a.

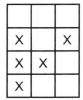

	X	
	X	
X	X	X

2b.

	X	
X	X	X
	X	

2c.

X		X
X	X	
X		

3. dance, paint, learn
4a. brain – game
4b. speak – meet
4c. time – find
5. none
6a. buy; It is not an artistic pursuit.
6b. sing; It is not a means of movement.
6c. bright; It is not a noun.

B

Answers will vary.

Unit 2: At school

Lesson A: Get ready
pages 19–21

A

1. Leticia speaks two languages. She is bilingual.
2. Hong wants to earn a lot of money. He needs a high-paying job.
3. Nassim wants to work in the tourism industry.
4. A good English test score is one of the program requirements.
5. The college offers financial aid to students who need money.
6. Fill out your application now. The deadline is tomorrow!

B

A: Good morning. Can I help you?
B: Yes, I'd like some information about the course requirements for one of your programs.
A: Yes, of course. Which program are you interested in?
B: Hospitality and Tourism.
A: You need to take three classes to get the certificate.
B: How much does it cost?
A: Each class costs $450.
B: Could you send me an application, please?
A: Yes, but you'll need to send it in right away. The deadline is next week.
B: OK. Thank you. Here is my address. . . .

C

Answers will vary.

Lesson B: The passive voice
pages 22–24

A

1. Free computer classes are provided in the summer.
2. The placement test is held in the library.
3. Are English classes offered, too?
4. What kind of experience is needed?
5. Is a certificate provided at the end?
6. What kind of forms are required?

B

1. Business classes are offered on Tuesdays and Thursdays.
2. A placement test is held on the first day of class.
3. Where is the admissions office located?
4. Is financial aid offered by the college?
5. Registration is required before March 15.
6. What kind of career advice is provided?

C

Answers will vary.

Lesson C: The passive voice
pages 25–27

A

1. Students are required to buy a textbook.
2. Students are expected to attend all the classes.
3. Students are advised to register early.
4. Students are told to meet with a tutor once a week.
5. Students are encouraged to hand in their homework on time.
6. Students are allowed to transfer credits from another program.

B

1. Are all students expected to take a placement test?
2. Is the college required to provide a test score?
3. Are students encouraged to send homework by e-mail?
4. Am I allowed to earn credits for work-experience programs?
5. Are students advised to speak with a counselor?
6. Is the teacher expected to give advice about study problems?

C

Answers will vary.

Lesson D: Reading pages 28–30

A

a. Ivana, Vacek
b. the Ukraine; the United States; Chicago, Illinois; Houston, Texas
c. 1990, 1992, 1994
d. programmer, junior clerk, manager, engineer

B

1. Where are Ivana and Vacek from? The Ukraine.
2. What did Ivana do before she came to the United States? She was a teacher.
3. Why did Ivana and Vacek decide to come to the United States? They needed more money.

4. Why did Ivana and Vacek move to Houston? Ivana got a better job.

C

Answers will vary.

Lesson E: Writing pages 31–33

A

1. What was Sandy's dream? He wanted to be a musician.
2. What three obstacles to success did Sandy have? He didn't have enough money for music lessons. His parents didn't encourage him. His friends didn't believe in him.
3. What did he do to overcome these obstacles? He saved money for music lessons. He practiced every day. He earned a scholarship to music school.
4. Why was Sandy successful? Because he had a dream and he never gave up.

B

1. Dave saved money for a new car. Success.
2. Sofia passed all her exams. Success.
3. Sam wasn't encouraged to study. Obstacle.
4. Luisa won a dance contest. Success.
5. Osman graduated from business school. Success.
6. Zhu wasn't offered a scholarship. Obstacle.

Lesson F: Another view
pages 34–36

A

1. offered
2. located
3. required
4. held
5. encouraged

B

1. statesman
2. writer
3. dancer
4. player
5. actor
6. musician
7. singer

Unit 3: Friends and Family

Lesson A: Get ready pages 37–39

A

1. My parents had a lot of rules. They were very strict.
2. I can tell my friend everything because I trust her.
3. We are not permitted to use cell phones in class.
4. I was born in Florida, but I was raised in California.
5. You can't go to the party alone. You need a chaperone.
6. Frieda copied her friend's homework. She broke the rules.

B

Soraya: My kids say that I'm too strict with them. Do you have rules for your kids, Amy?
Amy: Yes, we certainly do. I was brought up to understand that we need rules, and I'm raising my kids the same way.
Soraya: Are they permitted to stay out late?
Amy: No. They need to be home by 7:00 p.m. If they have a chaperone, they can stay out until 9:00 p.m., but no later.
Soraya: I see. And what kind of punishment do they get if they break the rules?
Amy: Let's see. They are grounded for the weekend . . . or no TV . . . or no cell phone – that's for something really serious.
Soraya: You have some good ideas! I'll have to try them with my kids.

C

Answers will vary.

Lesson B: Indirect questions
pages 40–42

A

1. Can you tell me why you are late?
2. I'd like to know where she went last night.
3. Tell me when you came home yesterday.
4. I wonder what he did yesterday.
5. Do you know how they are feeling now?
6. I don't know who they talked to after class.

B

1A. Do you know what his name is?
1B. His name is Jun.
2A. Can you tell me where the classroom is?
2B. The classroom is on the second floor.
3A. I don't know when the class starts.
3B. The class starts at 9:30 a.m.
4A. Tell me how you came to school this morning.
4B. I came to school by bus this morning.
5A. I wonder who they were talking to.
5B. They were talking to the teacher.
6A. I'd like to know why she got a D.
6B. She got a D because she didn't study very hard.

C

1. Can you tell me when she went home?
2. Do you know who the teacher is?
3. Tell me where the answers are.
4. I'd like to know when the test begins.
5. I don't know what they did in English class yesterday.
6. I wonder why she left school early today.

Lesson C: Indirect questions
pages 43–45

A

1. Can you tell me if I need to buy a ticket?
2. I'd like to know if I can bring my friend.
3. I wonder if all our classmates will be there.
4. Do you know if our teacher is invited?

5. Do you know if they are going to serve food?
6. I wonder if I need to bring soda or chips.

B

Sam: Hi, Penny. Did you hear about the class party?
Penny: No, I didn't. Do you know if it is this weekend?
Sam: No, it isn't this weekend. It's on Thursday.
Penny: I wonder if everyone in our class is going to be there.
Sam: Yes, everyone in our class is going to be there.
Penny: Do you know if there will be music?
Sam: Yes, I'm sure there will be music.
Penny: Good. Do you know if they had a party last year?
Sam: Yes, they had a party last year. It was fun. This party will be fun, too!

C

Answers will vary.

Lesson D: Reading pages 46–48
A

1. creative - adjective
2. education - noun
3. successful - adjective
4. communicate - verb
5. different - adjective

B

1. (a) a problem in communication
2. (a) technology
3. (b) designing video games
4. (a) he talks about things she doesn't understand

C

Answers will vary.

Lesson E: Writing pages 49–51
A

   One difference between Berta and her brother, Rob, is that they have different likes and dislikes. Berta likes sports. For example, she plays tennis at the gym every day. In addition, she likes to eat healthy food. For example, she often eats a banana on her way to work. She loves to wear nice clothes. For example, she often wears a suit to work. On the other hand, Rob is interested in computers. He goes on the Internet every day. He likes to eat junk food. For example, he loves cookies. He usually wears jeans and a T-shirt. Berta and Rob are very different. Maybe that's why they get along so well!

B

1. For example
2. On the other hand
3. For example
4. For example
5. On the other hand
6. On the other hand

C

Answers will vary.

Lesson F: Another view
pages 52–54
A

1. (a) adults in the U.S.
2. (a) 42 percent
3. (b) education
4. (b) More people chose money than education.

B

Names
Sheena
Diana
Jimmy
Martin

Unit 4: Health

Lesson A: Get ready pages 55–57
A

1. I feel upset and angry. I need to calm down.
2. Ariana feels nervous. She has a lot of anxiety.
3. I have too much work to do. I feel stressed out.
4. One way to relax is to practice deep breathing.
5. Lee has an exam. He feels nervous and tense.
6. Meditation is one way to cope with stress.

B

Do you feel stressed out? Do you feel worried and tense every day? Do you have trouble sleeping or concentrating at work? These are symptoms of stress in your life.
   Learn how to cope with stress in our easy meditation class. Learn techniques for deep breathing and thinking positive thoughts. Just ten minutes each day can help you calm down and relax. Learn to reduce anxiety. You'll enjoy life more!
   Classes start January 15. Call (304) 555-5689 to find out more.

C

1. People who feel stressed out.
2. You can't sleep and you can't concentrate.
3. Deep breathing and positive thinking.
4. Calm down and relax.
5. Answers will vary.

Lesson B: Modals pages 58–60
A

1. The deadline is next week. You don't have to register today.
2. Tomorrow is a holiday. We don't have to go to school.
3. Lisa starts work at 5:00 a.m. She has to wake up early.
4. Tony and Maria need a new car. They have to save money.
5. Ramona cooked a lot of food yesterday. She doesn't have to cook today.
6. I have a bad headache. I have to take some aspirin.

B

1A. I feel stressed out.
1B. You ought to do some meditation.
2A. I have a backache.
2B. You ought to see a doctor.
3A. I feel tired and sleepy all day.
3B. You shouldn't go to bed so late.
4A. I have too many bills.
4B. You shouldn't spend so much money.
5A. I don't have any friends.
5B. You ought to meet new people.

6A. I can't sleep at night.
6B. You shouldn't drink coffee.

C

1. George doesn't have to take the test today.
2. We have to learn how to relax.
3. Danny and Ming ought to register for school tomorrow.
4. Emiko shouldn't get so stressed out at work.
5. Terry and Linda don't have to buy a new car this year.
6. I should learn how to drive a car.

D

Answers will vary.

Lesson C: Modals pages 61–63

A

1. He overslept. He shouldn't have stayed up so late.
2. He skipped breakfast. He should have eaten breakfast.
3. He drove, but there was traffic. He should have taken the bus.
4. He forgot his ID. He should have remembered his ID.
5. He forgot his resume. He shouldn't have forgotten his resume.
6. He didn't bring all his papers. He should have brought all his papers.

B

1. She should have gotten up earlier.
2. She should have asked questions.
3. She should have talked to her co-workers.
4. She should have worn a suit.
5. She should have done some meditation.

C

Answers will vary.

Lesson D: Reading pages 64–66

A

1. stressful - adjective
2. reaction - noun
3. regularly - adverb
4. nervousness - noun
5. loosen - verb

B

1. Your knees shake and your throat feels dry.
2. We think that we have to be perfect.
3. It will help you to be well prepared and feel more confident.
4. It will relax your body and clear your mind.
5. How to stay calm when speaking in public.

Lesson E: Writing pages 67–69

A

1. depressed, depression
2. angry, anger
3. anxious, anxiety

B

1. When I feel depressed, I like talking with a friend. This helps me to get another opinion about my problems. Writing in my journal also helps me to think about why I feel sad.
2. When I feel angry, I like to take deep breaths and count to ten. This helps to reduce my blood pressure and stops me from saying something stupid.
3. When I feel anxious, I like to take a walk or listen to music. This helps me relax and think about something different. I also like to make a plan for the next day because that helps me feel more in control of my life.

C

Answers will vary.

Lesson F: Another view pages 70–72

A

1. (c) This chart is about how students cope with stress.
2. (a) The most popular way of managing stress was exercising or walking.
3. (b) The least popular way of managing stress was taking an over-the-counter medication.
4. (b) Watching TV was less popular than exercising or walking.

5. (c) Meditating or doing yoga was more popular than drinking alcohol.
6. (c) Eating candy or junk food was more popular than meditating or doing yoga.

B

1. Which was more popular – listening to music or playing video games? Playing video games.
2. Which was less popular – drinking alcohol or eating junk food? Drinking alcohol.
3. What percentage of the students exercise to manage stress? 45 percent.

Tier 3 questions and answers will vary.

Unit 5: Around town

Lesson A: Get ready pages 73–75

A

1. worthwhile   4. patient
2. coordinator   5. commitment
3. orientation   6. residents

B

Leo: Hi, Dave. Where are you going?
Dave: I'm going to my volunteer job at the local nursing home.
Leo: That sounds interesting. What do you do there?
Dave: I just talk to the residents and keep them company. It makes them feel better.
Leo: Is it difficult? I bet you have to be very patient.
Dave: It's not hard at all. And it feels good to do something worthwhile for other people.
Leo: Do you go every week?
Dave: Yes, I had to make a commitment of at least one hour a week when I started.
Leo: One hour a week isn't much. Do you think I could do that, too?
Dave: Sure! Why don't you come along and talk to the volunteer coordinator? Maybe you can come to the next orientation and find out more.

C

Answers will vary.

Lesson B: Time clauses
pages 76–78

A

1. As soon as I finish lunch, I'll take my medication.
2. Tina will work in the garden until it gets dark.
3. Adina will have her birthday lunch as soon as her family arrives.
4. As soon as I feel stronger, I'll start exercising again.
5. We will stay with you until visitors have to leave.
6. Stan and Frank will play cards until it is time for dinner.

B

1. As soon as they arrive, they'll have breakfast.
2. They'll have an orientation as soon as they finish breakfast.
3. They'll listen to introductions until the computer-skills class starts.
4. As soon as they finish the computer-skills class, they'll have lunch.
5. They'll use the Internet until lunch break is over.
6. They'll play sports with other volunteers as soon as lunch break is over.

C

Answers will vary.

Lesson C: Verb tense contrast
pages 79–81

A

1. once a week
2. twice a year
3. three times a year
4. twice a week
5. twice a month
6. three times a week

B

1. visited
2. have taken
3. cook
4. cleaned up
5. do
6. have collected

C

1. Adam took his neighbor to the doctor every week last year.
2. Flavia has delivered toys to children three times so far this year.
3. Anna and Gino read stories to children in the hospital once a month.
4. I have volunteered at the homeless shelter many times.
5. How often have you volunteered so far this year?
6. How many times did you volunteer last year?

D

Answers will vary.

Lesson D: Reading pages 82–84

A

1. insecure: not confident
2. grave: serious
3. impaired: damaged
4. tenacity: strength
5. gratifying: satisfying
6. rewarding: valuable

B

1. They help young people become confident.
2. They meet once a week.
3. He was lonely and insecure.
4. He admires his tenacity.
5. Volunteering is fun and worthwhile.

C

Answers will vary.

Lesson E: Writing pages 85–87

A

My brother, Andrew, and his wife, Lucy, are two of the most caring people I have ever met. They are eye doctors, and they have an eye clinic in Kansas City. Every year, they do something worthwhile to help other people. When patients come to the clinic to get new glasses, Andrew and Lucy ask them to donate their old glasses. Last year, they collected several hundred pairs of glasses. Then they spent two weeks working in a hospital in Calcutta, India. As soon as they arrived, people started to make a line in front of the hospital. Six hundred people got a free eye test and a free pair of glasses. It made a huge difference in their lives.

B

1. Who made a difference? Andrew and Lucy.
2. What did they do? Collected old glasses and gave them away.
3. Why did they do it? To help other people.
4. Where did this happen? In Kansas City and Calcutta, India.
5. When did it happen? Last year.
6. How did they make a difference? Six hundred people got a free eye test and a free pair of glasses.

C

Answers will vary.

Lesson F: Another view
pages 88–90

1. (b) You need to be at least 16 years old.
2. (b) You need to work 3 hours a week for six months.
3. (a) You need to attend an orientation session.
4. (b) You don't need any experience.
5. (a) Delivering toys, reading stories, and greeting visitors.

B

1. great
2. light
3. free
4. better

C

Answers will vary.

Unit 6: Time

Lesson A: Get ready pages 91–93

A

1. electronic
2. distracting
3. innovative
4. spam
5. convenient
6. text messages

B

1. A cell phone saves time because you don't need to look for a pay phone.

2. E-mail wastes time because you have to delete lots of spam.
3. A calculator saves time because you don't have to do math in your head.
4. A digital camera wastes time because you take too many pictures.
5. Using a computer saves time because it's faster than writing by hand.
6. The Internet saves time because you don't need to go to the library.

C

Answers will vary.

Lesson B: Clauses of concession pages 94–96

A

1. Even though I have a cell phone, I prefer to use e-mail.
2. Even though my brother lives nearby, I don't see him much.
3. Jerry prefers to write letters by hand even though he has e-mail at home.
4. Even though Steve has a car, he rides his bicycle to work every day.
5. Wanda doesn't want an air conditioner even though her house gets hot in summer.
6. Even though Olga loves watching movies, she doesn't want a DVD player.

B

1. Although she has a computer, she doesn't use the Internet at home.
2. Although she has a cell phone, she doesn't call me.
3. Although she has a DVD player, she goes to the movies a lot.
4. Although she has a dryer, she hangs her washing on the line.
5. Although she has an air conditioner, she uses a fan.
6. Although she has a dishwasher, she washes dishes in the sink.

C

Answers will vary.

Lesson C: Clauses of reason and concession pages 97–99

A

1. Although an electric oven takes longer, I prefer to cook with one.
2. Because an electronic dictionary is light, Jim keeps one in his backpack.
3. Although a dryer is noisy, Lucas uses one when he does laundry.
4. Because dishwashers use a lot of water, we wash our dishes by hand.
5. Because biking is good exercise, I bike to work.
6. Although I am an excellent cook, I usually eat out.

B

1. Although he has a car, Sam takes the subway to work.
2. Frank talks to his friends over the Internet because it is free.
3. Although they save a lot of time, I don't like electrical appliances.
4. Victor buys his lunch because he doesn't have time to make one at home.
5. Although it is faster by subway, Joe and Mei-Lin drive to work.
6. We often buy food online although it is more expensive.

C

Answers will vary.

Lesson D: Reading pages 100–102

A

1. amazing: fantastic
2. outrageous: very high
3. virtual: online
4. reasonable: not expensive
5. luckily: fortunately
6. popular: liked by a lot of people

B

1. What did Julia do for the first time? She bought groceries online.
2. Why didn't she try it before? She thought it was too expensive.
3. What did she find out about prices? They are very reasonable.
4. What did she think of the experience? She thought it was amazing.
5. What are the benefits? You can save time and it's easy.

Lesson E: Writing pages 103–105

A

1. cell phone: + convenient, – distracting
2. dishwasher: + easy to use, – noisy
3. MP3 player: + light, – expensive
Additional answers will vary.

B

My Favorite Time-saving Activity
    My favorite time-saving activity is online grocery shopping. Although I used to enjoy going to the store, it took a lot of time. I used to spend at least one evening a week on grocery shopping. Now I shop online. I save time because I don't have to drive to the store, and I don't have to wait in line. Another benefit of online shopping is that I can stick to my budget (and my diet!) because I don't buy cookies or chips. One disadvantage is that I have to wait one or two days for delivery. Another disadvantage is that delivery for orders under $100 is expensive.

Tier 3 answers will vary.

Lesson F: Another view
pages 106–108

A

1. (a) music
2. (b) electrical appliances
3. (b) music
4. (a) groceries
5. (b) airline tickets
6. (b) electrical appliances

B

Answers will vary.

Unit 7: Shopping

Lesson A: Get ready
pages 109–111

A

1. get my money back: get a refund
2. give back: return
3. buy: purchase
4. product: merchandise
5. does not work: is defective
6. rule: policy

B

Customer: Excuse me. Is this customer service?
Salesclerk: Yes. How can I help you?
Customer: I'd like to return this CD player. I'm not interested in an exchange.
Salesclerk: Is it defective?
Customer: No, it works fine. But it's just too complicated.
Salesclerk: Are you sure you don't want to exchange it for a different CD player?
Customer: No, thanks. Could I get a refund, please?
Salesclerk: I'm sorry. We don't give cash refunds. It's the store policy.
Customer: I see. Well, please give me a store credit instead.
Salesclerk: Could you please fill out this returned-merchandise form?

C

Answers will vary.

Lesson B: Adjective clauses
pages 112–114

A

1. I want to buy a camera that isn't very complicated.
2. I'd like to buy some jeans that aren't too expensive.
3. I usually go to the supermarket that is near my house.
4. The taxi driver who drove me home was very helpful.
5. Cell phones that ring loudly are very annoying.
6. The clerks who work at the computer store are very polite.

B

1. Terry wants to buy a laptop that is not too heavy.
2. The store that is near my house sells discount furniture.
3. The salesclerk who sold you this handbag is not here today.
4. The cameras that are in the window are on sale.
5. Most people want to buy computers that have a flat screen.
6. I like supermarkets that have a lot of good discounts.

C

Answers will vary.

Lesson C: Adjective clauses
pages 115–117

A

1. damaged / The DVDs that I received as a gift were damaged.
2. torn / The book that I borrowed from the library was torn.
3. defective / The toaster that I bought at Dave's Electrical Store was defective.
4. too small / The shoes that I ordered from a catalog were too small.
5. broken / The cup that I picked up at a garage sale was broken.

B

1. The oranges that I bought yesterday were spoiled.
2. The camera that you sold me last week doesn't work.
3. The book that I need for my math class is very expensive.
4. The man that I met last week wants to buy my car.
5. I can't find the dictionary that I borrowed from the library.

C

Answers will vary.

Lesson D: Reading pages 118–120

A

1. a book lover
2. a time limit
3. a store credit
4. a cash refund
5. a return policy

B

Dear Smart Shopper,
   I am a book lover, and I purchased some used books. Later, I found that two books had torn pages. I took them back, but the seller said that he didn't have to give me a cash refund because I bought them more than 28 days ago. He agreed to give me a store credit. Why can't I get my money back?
Angry Arnold

Dear Angry Arnold,
   If the product is new and you find it is defective, you can ask for a refund. For used merchandise, it's the buyer's responsibility to check it carefully before buying. There may also be a time limit for returns, so you should not wait. Always read the information on your receipt about the retailer's return policy.
Smart Shopper

C

1. Arnold was angry because his books were damaged.
2. He did not know that there was a time limit on returns.
3. The seller did not want to give Arnold a cash refund.
4. The seller gave Arnold a store credit.
5. He should read the receipt to learn about the return policy.

Lesson E: Writing pages 121–123

A

Why you should use a credit card
You can pay later.
You don't need cash.
You get a record of your purchases.
Additional answers will vary.

Why you shouldn't use a credit card
You can spend too much.
You get a large bill once a month.
You pay a lot of interest.
Additional answers will vary.

B

1. First 3. Next
2. Second 4. Finally

C

Example answer:
Why You Shouldn't Use a
Credit Card

There are some good reasons
why you shouldn't use a credit
card when you go shopping. First,
you can spend too much. Second,
you get a large bill once a month.
Next, you pay a lot of interest.
Finally, you could lose your card
and someone else might start
using it.

Lesson F: Another view
pages 124–126

A

1. (a) She will get a cash refund.
2. (b) He will get a store credit.
3. (b) He will get no refund.
4. (b) She will get a refund
by check.

B

1. (c) Yes, it cost a fortune.
2. (a) No, it was marked down.
3. (d) Yes, I had to shop around
for it.
4. (b) No, it's a real lemon.

Unit 8: Work

Lesson A: Get ready
pages 127–129

A

1. find a solution: work it out
2. the first letters of your name:
your initials
3. very tired: exhausted
4. reach an agreement: negotiate
5. take responsibility for: deal
with
6. part: share

B

1A. Did you reach an agreement
with your customer?
1B. No, I didn't. I'll have to
negotiate with him again
tomorrow.

2A. Are you going to tell your
boss about the problem?
2B. No, I'm going to try to work
it out with my co-worker
first.
3A. I always do more work than
you!
3B. No, you don't. I always do my
share.
4A. My co-worker always leaves
work early. What should I do?
4B. You should ask your boss to
deal with it.
5A. What is the chart for?
5B. We have to write our job
duties and our initials on it.
6A. How are you feeling today?
6B. I'm completely exhausted.

C

Answers will vary.

Lesson B: Tense contrast
pages 130–132

A

1. Luisa has been doing her
homework for 30 minutes.
2. Mary has been talking on the
phone for 15 minutes.
3. Louisa has done her
homework.
4. Mary has finished talking on
the phone.
5. Pete has been cooking dinner
for 40 minutes.
6. Pete has finished cooking
dinner.
7. Pete, Luisa, and Mary have
been eating dinner for
10 minutes.
8. Pete, Luisa, and Mary have
eaten dinner.

B

1. Pam has been baking bread for
two hours.
2. Gino and Teresa have been
cleaning the windows for
one hour.
3. We have just opened the front
door of the store.
4. Tam and Luis have finished
eating breakfast.

5. I have been talking on the
phone for 20 minutes.
6. Sonya has just arrived
at work.

C

Answers will vary.

Lesson C: Participial adjectives
pages 133–135

A

1. excited 4. frustrated
2. disappointed 5. frightened
3. bored 6. fascinated

B

1. interesting 5. exciting
2. tiring 6. disappointing
3. boring 7. exhausted
4. irritated 8. amused

C

Answers will vary.

Lesson D: Reading pages 136–138

A

Hard job skills
Can fix equipment
Can use a computer
Speaks other languages
Is good at math

Soft job skills
Arrives on time
Is honest
Is friendly
Is good at talking to people

B

1. Has good communication
skills / She is always friendly
and polite to the customers.
2. Has a strong work ethic / She
is always on time for work and
always finishes her tasks.
3. Learns from criticism / When
her boss criticizes her, she
doesn't complain.
4. Has a positive attitude / She's
always cheerful and optimistic.
5. Is a team player / Eugenia
gets along well with her
co-workers, too.

A

```
                                    Eugenia Chang
                                    458 North Main St.
                                    Providence, RI 02906
                                    August 8, 2008
Edmilson Ferreira, Sports Coordinator
Capital Athletics
356 Farmington Ave.
Hartford, CT 06108

Dear Mr. Ferreira,
    I read your advertisement online for a
position as a sports instructor. I am very
interested in this position, and I have enclosed
my resume.
    I have been working as a front desk
manager at Island Sports for 18 months. In this
job, I have learned how to help customers use
the sports equipment. I am skilled at teaching
many sports. I also get along well with my
co-workers.
    I am looking for an opportunity to learn
more and take on more responsibility in my job.
I look forward to hearing from you.
                                    Sincerely,
                                    Eugenia Chang
                                    Eugenia Chang
```

B

Example answer:

```
                                    Julio Alvarez
                                    5 Elk Dr.
                                    Cranston, RI 02921
                                    August 8, 2008
Margery Vincent, Manager
Island Sports Club
P.O. Box 4567
Providence, RI 02903

Dear Ms. Vincent:
    I read your advertisement for a position as a
front desk manager. I am very interested in this
position, and I have enclosed my resume.
    I have been working as a coach at Cole
High School for two years. In this job, I have
learned how to work well with young people. I
am skilled at coaching volleyball and baseball.
I enjoy helping people, and I have a positive
attitude.
    I am looking for an opportunity to learn
more and take on more responsibility in my job.
I look forward to hearing from you.
                                    Sincerely,
                                    Julio Alvarez
                                    Julio Alvarez
```

Lesson F: Another view
pages 142–144

A

1. (d) verbal communication
2. (b) manage time
3. (e) written communication
4. (a) understand directions
5. (c) reading comprehension
6. (g) strong work ethic
7. (f) teach others
8. (d) verbal communication
9. (b) manage time

B

1. written communication
2. manage time
3. reading comprehension
4. teach others
Tier 3 answers will vary.

C

Answers will vary.

Unit 9: Daily living

Lesson A: Get ready
pages 145–147

A

1. protect
2. recycle
3. responsibility
4. energy-efficient
5. global
6. cut down on

B

Find Out More About Living Green

Do you want to protect the environment? Not sure what to do? Come to the Living Green informational talk to find out more. Learn about some simple steps to cut down on energy use, including:
• how to buy energy-efficient appliances
• how to start a carpool club
• how to recycle bottles, cans, and clothing
It's time to take responsibility for saving the earth from global warming!
Gates Public Library, Thursday 6:00–7:00 p.m. All welcome.

C

1. Use energy-efficient appliances.
2. Carpool with co-workers.
3. Recycle your glass and paper.
Additional answers will vary.

Lesson B: Conditional sentences pages 148–150

A

1. reduce energy use, reduce trash
2. recycle newspapers, recycle plastic
3. tune up your car, tune up your engine
4. save gas, save water
5. fix water leaks, fix your car
6. replace lightbulbs, replace tires
Tier 3 answers will vary.

B

1. (e) If everyone carpooled to work, the roads would be less crowded.
2. (d) Frank would save money on gas if he took the bus to work.
3. (f) If people recycled their paper, we would save trees.
4. (c) You would cut down on trash if you used recycled paper.
5. (a) If I took shorter showers, I would save water.
6. (b) Sasha would use less electricity if she replaced her lightbulbs.

C

1. If you used less plastic, you would reduce trash.
2. If drivers checked their tires more often, they would save gas.
3. You would help the environment if you bought less plastic.
4. People would save electricity if they replaced their lightbulbs.
5. Jan would use less water if she took shorter showers.
6. If everyone picked up their trash, the beach would be cleaner.

D

Answers will vary.

Lesson C: Connectors
pages 151–153

A

1. The oceans are getting warmer. The ice caps are melting.
2. People are cutting down trees. Animals and birds have fewer places to live.
3. We are using up gas and oil. We will need other sources of energy.
4. The sea level is rising. Islands are sinking.
5. There is not enough rain. People cannot grow as much food.
6. The world population is growing. Cities are getting larger.

B

1. The oceans are getting warmer. As a result, the ice caps are melting.
2. Since people are cutting down trees, animals and birds have fewer places to live.
3. We are using up gas and oil. Consequently, we will need other sources of energy.
4. The sea level is rising. As a result, islands are sinking.
5. Since there is not enough rain, people cannot grow as much food.
6. The world population is growing. Consequently, cities are getting larger.

C

1. Due to
2. Consequently
3. As a result
4. Since

Tier 3 answers will vary.

Lesson D: Reading pages 154–156

A

1. race: competition
2. replied: answered
3. route: a direction to travel
4. swiftly: quickly
5. peacefully: quietly
6. approach: get nearer

B

1. He was slow.
2. They decided to have a race.
3. He took a nap.
4. He continued slowly but surely.

Tier 3 answers will vary.

C

(a) The fastest is not always the winner.

Tier 3 answers will vary.

Lesson E: Writing pages 157–159

A

1. Plastic bags are light and easy to carry. Customers prefer them.
2. Stores give away bags for free. Customers don't reuse them.

3. Customers throw the bags away. There are too many bags in the trash.
4. There is a huge amount of plastic in the ground. Chemicals get into the soil and the water.

B

The Causes and Effects of Too Many Plastic Bags

We use too many plastic bags, and it is a serious environmental problem. One cause is that plastic bags are light and easy to carry. As a result, customers prefer them. Another cause is that stores give away plastic bags for free. Consequently, customers don't reuse them. Since customers throw the plastic bags away, there are too many bags in the trash. Due to the huge amount of plastic in the ground, chemicals get into the soil and the water. If we used fewer plastic bags, we would cause less damage to the environment.

C

Answers will vary.

Lesson F: Another view pages 160–162

A

1. efficient
2. pollution
3. global
4. energy
5. recycle
6. environmental

B

Save energy at home
Don't use air-conditioning.
Turn down your heater.
Use energy-efficient lightbulbs.
Turn out the lights.

Save gas
Carpool to work.
Share a car with your neighbor.
Take the bus or the train.
Ride a bicycle.

Save water
Take shorter showers.
Use the dishwasher only when it is full.
Don't leave water running.
Don't water your grass.

Unit 10: Leisure

Lesson A: Get ready
pages 163–165

A

1. tradition
2. symbolizes
3. acquaintances
4. reception
5. courses
6. forward

B

1. The guests throw rice at the newly married couple. False.
2. The color red symbolizes good fortune. True.
3. Traditionally only family members are invited to the wedding ceremony. True.
4. The party usually includes a dinner with four courses. False.
5. It is a tradition that guests give money to the bride and groom. True.
6. The bride and groom are usually registered for gifts at a store. False.

C

Answers will vary.

Lesson B: Conditional sentences pages 166–168

A

1. If I go shopping tomorrow, I'll spend too much money.
2. If Sue had more free time, she would listen to music more often.
3. They won't eat dinner outside if the weather is cold.
4. We would invite all our friends over if our house were bigger.
5. If you didn't stay up so late, you wouldn't feel so tired.
6. I'll wear my new shirt if I go to the party.

B

1. If the weather is warm, she will go to the beach. If she stays home, she will make dinner with friends.
2. If they watch the fireworks, they will stay out until the next morning. If they were at home in Seattle, they would go to bed at midnight.

3. If our friends come over, we will go to a club later in the evening. If we weren't at our parents' house, we would invite all our friends over for a party.
4. If the weather isn't too cold, I will walk to a bar to listen to live music. If I didn't live in the center of Boston, I would have to drive to the bar.

C

Answers will vary.

Lesson C: Expressing hopes and wishes pages 169–171

A

1. Ronnie hopes his son comes / will come home for Thanksgiving.
2. Elena wishes her friends would call her more often.
3. Francisco hopes his parents will buy / buy him a cell phone for his birthday.
4. Tam wishes he could buy a new car.
5. Katrina hopes her mother will bake / bakes some cookies next weekend.
6. Maya and Alex wish they could take a vacation.

B

1. We hope all our friends come / will come to our wedding party.
2. Frank and Ella hope their children will visit / visit them this weekend.
3. Pamela hopes her boyfriend will take / takes her out for dinner.
4. My sister wishes she had a bigger house.
5. Marta and Juan wish their parents would visit them in the United States.
6. My wife wishes I would give her flowers more often.

C

Answers will vary.

Lesson D: Reading pages 172–174

A

1. branches: pieces of a tree
2. sticky: stays together
3. shows: concerts
4. cast: throw
5. offered: given

B

1. What is a New Year food in Japan? Sticky rice cakes.
2. What is a "bonenkai"? An end-of-year party.
3. What do people hear at midnight in Japan? A temple bell.
4. What gifts do Brazilians give to the water goddess? Flowers, perfume, or rice.
5. What is the "first footing"? The first visitor.
6. What do people in Scotland offer to their visitors? A small glass of whiskey.
7. What is "Auld Lang Syne"? A traditional song in Scotland.

Lesson E: Writing pages 175–177

A

A: My favorite celebration is the Fourth of July.
B: This holiday is also known as Independence Day.
People celebrate winning independence from Great Britain.
C: It is also a day when friends and family get together.
We decorate our homes with the American flag.
In the morning, we usually see a parade in the neighborhood streets.
For lunch, we usually have a barbecue or picnic in the park.
At night, there is a big fireworks show with music.
D: I like the Fourth of July because it is a summer celebration that lasts all day.

B

My Favorite Celebration
My favorite celebration is the Fourth of July. This holiday is also known as Independence

Day. People celebrate winning independence from Great Britain. It is also a day when friends and family get together. We decorate our homes with the American flag. In the morning, we usually see a parade in the neighborhood streets. For lunch, we usually have a barbecue or picnic in the park. At night, there is a big fireworks show with music. I like the Fourth of July because it is a summer celebration that lasts all day.

C

Answers will vary.

Lesson F: Another view pages 178–180

A

1. When is New Year's Eve? December 31.
2. When is Independence Day? July 4.
3. What is the traditional food on Thanksgiving? Turkey.
4. What do people usually do on Valentine's Day? Give flowers and chocolates to someone they love.
5. When is April Fools' Day? April 1.

B

1. Preheat the oven to 350°F. Mix the flour, baking powder, and salt in a bowl.
2. Melt the butter and chocolate over hot water or very low heat.
3. In a second bowl, beat the eggs. Add the sugar to the eggs a little at a time.
4. Mix in the chocolate and butter mixture. Stir in the flour mixture and blend well.
5. Stir in chopped nuts and vanilla.
6. Pour into an 8-inch square pan. Bake at 350° for about 25 minutes.
7. Cool in the pan and cut into squares. Serve with ice cream.

Illustration credits

Chuck Gonzales: 13, 14, 15, 61, 62, 63, 154, 155, 156
John Batten: 34, 35, 36, 103, 104, 105, 115, 116, 117, 178, 179, 180
Monika Roe: 19, 20, 21, 55, 56, 57, 130, 131, 132, 178, 179, 180
William Waitzman: 49, 50, 51, 67, 68, 69, 169, 170, 171

Notes

Notes

Notes